Understanding Biblical Principles

LIVING A LIFE WITH MEANING AND SIGNIFICANCE

DANIEL ASIHENE

Copyright © 2020 by Daniel Asihent. All rights reserved.

Requests for information should be addressed to:
apostlekadaniel@gmail.com

This book, or parts thereof, may not be reproduced, stored in a retrieval system, or transmitted in any form or by any means, electronic, mechanical, photocopying, recording or otherwise, without the written permission of the publisher.

Published By: Achievers World Publishing

ISBN: 978-0-6487534-3-8 (Paperback)
ISBN: 978-0-6487534-4-5 (ebook)

Unless otherwise stated, scripture quotations are from the New King James Version (NKJV) of the Bible.
Printed in Australia

DEDICATION

I dedicate this book in loving memory of my beloved late pastor and mother, Pastor Hattie B. Thompkins, who taught me through word and deed who God is and how to begin to posture myself toward Him.

Table of Contents

Acknowledgement 1

Foreword 2

Introduction 5

Part One 11

Chapter 1: How We Got The Bible 12

Chapter 2: The Bible Translation 26

Part Two 39

Chapter 3: Who Is Jesus? 40

Chapter 4: Jesus In The Old Testament 48

Chapter 5: Jesus In The Tabernacle 58

Chapter 6: Why Jesus Was Manifested 74

Chapter 7: Jesus Healing Wings 101

Chapter 8: The Reality Of God's Grace 112

Chapter 9: Locating Yourself In Prophecy 123

Chapter 10: Gift 141

ACKNOWLEDGEMENT

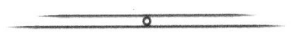

This knowledge and revelation was revealed to me by the Holy Spirit, for it is impossible to write a book like this without the help of some divine connections. I therefore thank God for His wisdom and grace towards me.

Secondly I would like to thank Manana my wife and the family for their undivided moral and material support they gave towards this project.

Pastor Femi Oyewopo, the CEO of Achievers World Publishing understands my heart. As my publisher, Achievers World Publishing organised my words and made them come alive. Thank you, Pastor Femi, for the passionate work of your team on "UNDERSTANDING BIBLICAL PRINCIPLES."

Mr Trevor Bongani Zungu, my brother-in-law, Dr. and Mrs Assibey Bonsu, Dr. and Mrs Fornah, Pastor and Mrs Baloyi, Pastor Shalom, Sis. Dorcas Tubei, Mr Andrew and Hope Kachila, Dr Kai Jochen Nalder and Dorcas Abena Wilkes, not forgetting Grace Outreach Church, I say God richly bless you all for your encouragement and prayer support.

FOREWORD

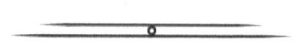

Although the world continues to resist God and the resistance mutates, the Lord God also continues to circumvent the ways of the enemy (Satan) by raising men and women who have made themselves available to receiving in-depth divine revelations which when told will enable us to have understanding, which hitherto was not very clear in perspective. Apostle Daniel is one of such persons, devoted to spewing out God's wisdom and revelations to liberate the confused world of lingering doubts of our understanding of the word of God. This treatise, I believe, will help give us an inner elucidation to understand a little bit more of the will of God for our lives.

I humbly urge you to read it, assimilate and live by it. May God richly bless the writer and anyone who reads this book.

Rev.Dr.Michael Twum-Darko - Minister Provincial- African Province,Priest-in-charge, Church of Holy Redeemer,Sea Point- Cape Town. Ghana Consular, Cape Town.

I have read Apostle Daniel's book "Understanding Biblical Principles", and of a truth it is a must read book. I therefore recommend that Christians and non-Christians grab copies and read this book for their own benefit. Be blessed as you read along.

Rev.Dr. Andrew Ankrah
Principal,Christian Bible College,Accra,Ghana.

In this book, Pastor Daniel Asihene presents a clear answer to many questions, believers and unbelievers alike, have about what the bible is all about.

He explains how the Bible came into existence and some of the principles it contains for a good and godly lifestyle.

This book is easy to understand, gives a great overview and has many illustrations from the author's life and ministry that help root the principles into daily life.

If you would like to know more about the Bible, dig deep into this book. I am confident you will find something to help you in your journey.

Wendy Yapp
A product of Glasgow University and Glasgow's Bible Training Institute.
Director of PrayerCare International. Perth,Western Australia.

It was a great privilege to have met Pastor Daniel Asihene of Grace Outreach Church at a meeting of pastors wanting to see the gospel reach nations. I believe God has inspired this noble minister of the gospel to put together his thought on the God's biblical principles.

Many Christians today seem to under-estimate the biblical principles of God which are His covenant and regulations that creation should follow. Satan will arrange circumstances and use believers in the same faith to stop the gift God had given each individual in order to break the rules. I also believe that this book has addressed what the Bible is and how we got it, the truth and the power that the bible contains. The word of God includes many examples on how to rightly divide the word of truth and apply it positively to obtain positive results. God's principles are made mentioned in several places in the bible; Revelation 1:5 "And from Jesus Christ, who is the faithful witness..." Through this book and by the inspired power of the Holy Spirit, every believer will understand the principles of God to the set rules and regulations that creation should follow. May the Lord continue to have steadfast minds, Isaiah 26:3.

Rev.Dr.Francis Obed Fornah
Snr.Overseer G.R.A.C.E Ministries Int'l Inc.
Winner of Community awards for being pro- active in the Christian faith.
Author of Unanswered questions in Christendom.
Perth,Western Australia.

INTRODUCTION

In time past God created a beautiful garden called Eden, gave it to man to keep it, and attached to it were principles on how Adam was supposed to govern the garden, but he failed woefully because he was unable to apply the principles pertaining to the garden.

God who is rich in mercy, decided to restore man back to glory, so He came down on earth in the form of a man called Jesus (Immanuel, God with us). God in His manifold wisdom again has laid before man principles which could be found in His written word (the Bible), and He expects creation to comply with these principles and enjoy life, but failure to do so will see one's life fizzled out completely.

God's inconceivable love has also provided for mankind everything pertaining to his success in life. Therefore, there is no way a believer should fail; it is unacceptable and against divine order. What the believer ought to do is to search the scriptures and understand how these principles of God work and apply them accordingly because the believer is expected to live a life with meaning and significance due to the new creation concept as recorded in 2 Corinthians 5:17.

However, there is an accuser of the brethren, the devil, the father of all lies who works hard to ensure that man violates these principles so that he would be rejected and destroyed as he did in the garden of Eden. My candid advice for you beloved is to have a copy of this book, read it and understand how the biblical principles work. For many have the zeal for God's work but not according to knowledge and because of that have been caught in the devil's web unknowingly. The adversary is trying to turn some of the churches into a synagogue of Satan (charismatic gymnastics), especially places where ignorance reigns supreme. The present generation is gradually giving way to deceiving spirits and doctrines of demons, speaking lies and hypocrisy (heresies). The adversary in his cunning tactics is swaying many and even the elect from the bible, for he knows that it is only the truth (the Bible)that can make mankind free - John 8:32.

One can see the old and the young, men and women trooping to prayer and church services without a bible, lest to say having new convert classes or baptismal classes. Most of these leaders who founded these churches and prayer ministries are prophets who cannot read or write, and in such cases, how can they preach or teach about the Saviour. Can a blind man lead his fellow blind man? Certainly not!

I always say this, if the medical doctor or the legal practitioner can study medicine or law for many years to become a qualified medical doctor or lawyer, how come some men of God spend three months or even less to become pastors and spiritual leaders. If the medical practitioner has to spend many years to be able to take care of a body which eventually goes back to the dust, how come some pastors spend three months to take care of a soul that moves on to eternity. With a situation like this, will the heathens respect and take us seriously?

As one of God's generals, I would like to use this medium to appeal to anyone who gets a copy of this book to make a good decision and go back to the bible, for salvation, peace, freedom or prosperity are not found outside the word of God.

The book addresses what the Bible is and how we got it, the truth and the power that the bible contains, how to rightly divide the word of truth, and apply them to obtain positive results. The book also addresses how the believer can live a life with meaning and significance. The principles of Jesus Christ create our prosperity and prepare us for the earth, while the person of Jesus prepares us for eternity. Beloved any act which has not got any biblical support or foundation must be rejected. You are born original, do not die a copy.

THE FOLLOWING WERE NOTABLE SAYING ABOUT THE BIBLE.

"I believe the Bible is the best gift God has ever given to man. All the good from the Saviour of the world is communicated to us through this book."

— Abraham Lincoln

"I have known ninety-five of the wold's great men in my time, and of these eighty-seven were followers of the Bible. The Bible is stamped with a specialty of origin, and an immeasurable distance separates it from all competitors."

— W.E.Gladstone

"It is impossible to rightly govern the world without God and the Bible."

— George Washington.

"The Bible is no mere book, but a living creature with a power that conquers all that opposes it."

— Napoleon.

"That book accounts for the supremacy of England."

— Queen Victoria

"If there is anything in my thoughts or style to commend, the credit is due to my parents for instilling in me an early love of the scriptures. If we abide by the principles taught in the Bible, our country will go on prospering and to prosper, but if we and our posterity neglect it's instructions and authority, no man can tell how sudden a catastrophe may overwhelm us and bury all our glory in profound obscurity."

— Daniel Webster

"The whole of human progress is suspended on the ever-growing influence of the Bible."

— W.H. Seward

"The Bible is worth all other books which have ever been printed."

— Patrick Henry

"The Bible is the sheet anchor of our liberties."

— U.S. Grant

"It is impossible to enslave mentally or socially a bible-reading people. The principles of the bible are the groundwork of human freedom."

— **Horace Greeley**

"The book, Sir, is the rock on which our republic rests."

— **Andrew Jackson**

"In all my perplexities and distresses, the bible has never failed to give me light and strength."

— **Robert E. Lee**

"Bible reading is an education itself."

— **Lord Tennyson**

"So great is my veneration for the bible that the earlier my children began to read it, the more confident will be my hope that they will prove useful citizens of their country and responsible members of society. I have for many years made it a practice to read through the bible once every year."

— **John Quincy Adams**

"The existence of the bible, as a book for the people, is the greatest benefit that the human race has ever experienced. Every attempt to belittle it is a crime against humanity."

— **Immanuel Kant**

"The New Testament Is The Very Best Book That Ever Was Or Ever Will Be Known In The World."

— **Charles Dickens**

"There are sure marks of authenticity in the bible than in any profane history."

— **Sir Isaac Newton**

"Let mental culture go on advancing, let the natural sciences progress in ever greater extent and depth, and the human mind widen itself as much as it desires beyond the elevation and moral culture of Christianity as it shines forth in the gospels, it will not go."

— **Goethe**

PART ONE

CHAPTER 1

HOW WE GOT THE BIBLE

Once a Muslim brother asked me, "why Jesus has to die before someone could be saved." I then used Romans 8:11 to explain to him, and he was amazed to hear that. It is, therefore, a principle for every human being to believe in the blood of Jesus to be saved. I also asked him why would he put petrol into his car instead of water because water is far cheaper compared to petrol, and again why would he eat through the mouth instead of the nose? It was an interesting debate, but thank God; the Muslim brother is now a Christian.

There are principles behind everything that God created, and He expects creation to be in accordance with these principles to enjoy an abundant life.

What Then Is A Principle?

"It is the fundamental or basic idea or rule that explains or control how something works or happens."

— **Cambridge English Dictionary.**

"A basic belief, theory or rule that has a major influence on the way in which something is done."

— **Mac Millan Dictionary.**

"A rule that explains how something works. A rule that is very important and that should not be broken."

— **Longman Dictionary Of Contemporary English.**

"Principles are rules or laws that are permanent, unchanging, and universal in nature."

— **By Keith Norris, CEO Of Complete XRM, INC (Planplusonline).**

My Definition Of Principles

"Principles are permanent unchanging universal rules or regulations (call it laws and you will not be far from right) which the creator of the universe (God Almighty) has provided or set down to guide or govern nature, showing how something works or happens."

The above definitions of principles show that:

- Principles are permanent, unchanging and universal.
- Principles are rules and regulations that have been set down by the creator of the universe, and He expects nature to comply with them.
- Principles cannot be broken.
- Principles determine how a thing works or happens.

What Is Understanding?

According to Cambridge English Dictionary, understanding means to have knowledge about a subject, situation or to know how something works.

The Greek word for understanding is "Sunesis " meaning the ability to understanding concepts and see relationships between them, or knowing the meaning of an accumulated information or truth.

When the meaning of information is not known or understood, one is tantamount to wrong application of the information or truth. In **1 Corinthians .2:8**, the scripture says *"none of the rulers of this age knew; for had they known, they would not have crucified the Lord of glory."*

The information, the truth (the Old Testament) was available to them but they lacked the meaning (understanding) of the scriptures (information) and therefore applied the information they had wrongly.

Let me also say that the principles of Jesus Christ create prosperity for the believer, enabling him to live a life with meaning and significance, whilst the person Jesus creates eternal life.

In **Proverbs 24:3-4 GNV**, the scripture says "homes are built on the foundation of wisdom and understanding. Where there is knowledge, the rooms are furnished with valuable, beautiful things.". Knowledge, understanding and wisdom are the foundation of every goal the scripture says.

For a person to live a life with meaning, significance and prosperity, he or she must first know the meaning of God's principles (understanding) to enable the person apply the principles (the knowledge) rightly (wisdom).

What Does Biblical Means?

It means Relating to or contained in the Bible-Cambridge English Dictionary.

When I was young, I thought that Jerusalem, Israel, Egypt, the Garden of Eden, and their likes were cities, nations in heaven, but little did I know that they are all here on earth.

Have you ever asked yourself or someone the following questions such as:

- How we got the Bible and where it came from?
- Who wrote the Bible?
- Is the Bible truly God's word?
- Is the Bible not a storybook?
- When was the Bible written?

The Bible

The English word Bible comes from "biblia" in Latin and "biblos" in Greek. The term means book or books which originally described papyrus-an ancient writing material made from reeds that grow along the Nile river in Egypt.

The bible is the inspired word of God, an accurate eyewitness account of history that says everything. It is the authority for Christian life and practice, and a foundation on which believers must build their thinking.

The bible is a devoted collection of sixty-six books, written by about forty different authors over a period of 1500 years. Some of these authors were Shepherds, farmers, tax collectors, fishermen, rabbis, and kings. Most importantly, the Bible has one author - God Himself. The bible is God-breathed 2Timothy 3:16, and its human authors wrote exactly what God wanted them to write, and the result was the perfect and holy word of God - Psalm 12:6, 2Peter 1:21.

The bible is God's way of telling us about Himself, His nature, attributes, plans, and purpose. The Old Testament begins with the first five Books of Moses, which is the Pentateuch (the Torah) Genesis-Deuteronomy; the Historical books are from Joshua-Esther, the Poetical books are from Job-Song of Solomon, and the prophetical books are from Isaiah-Malachi, which add up to 39 books.

The New Testament tells the story of how God sent His begotten son, Jesus, to save mankind from sin. It begins with the four Gospels, Matthew, Mark, Luke, and John, the accounts of the life of Christ, and continues with a historical book - Acts of the Apostles. From Romans to Jude are the letters (Epistles), then the book of Revelation, the prophetic book, which explains how the world will end and what will happen to the people of the world.

The bible begins with the story of creation, how God created the universe, and then placed mankind on the earth to subdue it. Mankind rebelled, choosing to reject God and follow their own desires. God knowing this would happen, already had a plan in place to renew His fellowship with mankind so God gave a single nation Israel, a set of laws to follow and encourage other nations to follow, but this could not work according to God's plan. Israel totally failed God. After many years of rejecting God's law, God exiled Israel away from their homeland.

When the stage was set, and the people understood better how much they needed God's presence, God sent His son, with the full deity of God and a full humanity of man (John 1:14, John 8:58, John 10:30), to personally interact with Israel, as described in the Gospel account.

Jesus explained that what was true for the nation of Israel was true for every individual on the planet. Obeying God and His laws was impossible, and therefore, a mediator was necessary to bridge the gap between sinful man and a holy God. Jesus Christ, the perfect lamb of God, made this reconciliation possible through His perfect sacrifice on the cross for sin. He personally took the weight of sin and our separation from God, giving everyone who accepted by faith His sacrifice the ability to return to the full presence of God. Jesus was sinless and because of that God accepted His sacrifice, He rose from the dead three days later, conquering death for all who choose Him.

To explain these things to the rest of the world, God established a more varied ambassador than a single nation-He created the CHURCH. As the word of Jesus sacrifice spread, church leaders wrote letters explaining more fully what Jesus had done, what He meant, and how to follow Him. This could be found in Romans - Jude.

The New Testament ends with a prophetic revelation. It was the impact the church would have on the world, the final rejection of Jesus by the world, and God's judgement on the world. Church leaders gathered the accounts of Jesus, the historical book, the letters, and the prophecy, and after many years of discussion and research settled on the 27 books of the New Testament that we have today.

Facts About The Bible
What The Bible Is:

The bible is God's inspired revelation of the origin and destiny of all things. It is the traveller's map, the pilgrim's staff, the pilot's compass, the soldier's sword, and the Christian charter. The bible is the power of God unto eternal salvation and the source of present help for body, soul, and spirit. Christ is the grand subject. It is a mine of wealth, the source of health and a world of pleasure. The bible is God's will or testament to men of all ages, revealing the plan of God for man here now, and in the next life. It will be opened at the judgement, and it will last forever.

The bible is God's dealings with man in the past, present, and future. It contains His message of eternal salvation for all who believe in Christ and eternal damnation for all who rebel against the Gospel.

The bible is the only book that reveals the mind of God, the state of man, the way of salvation, the doom of sinners and the happiness of believers. Its doctrines are holy, its precepts are binding, its histories are true, and its decisions are immutable. It contains light to direct, spiritual food to sustain, and comfort to cheer. Man should read it to be wise, believe it to be saved, and practice it to be holy. Man should read it that it might fill his memory, rule his heart, and rule his feet in righteousness. Man should read it slowly, frequently, prayerfully, meditatively, devotionally, study it constantly until it becomes a part of his being, generating faith that will move mountains.

What The Bible Is Not:

The bible is not an amulet, a charm, a fetish, or anything to work wonders by its very presence alone. It does not claim to be such. It does claim that if one will study and practice its teachings he will see wonders worked in his life both now and the hereafter.

The bible is not a book of chronological events or an unbroken series of divine utterances. It was given here a little and there a little - Isaiah 28:9-11.

The bible is not a book of heavenly utterances in supernatural language, it is God's revelation in the most simple human language possible.

The bible is not a book adapted to the tastes, customs, and habits of any nation or people. It is not for any age or period of time. It is a book into which all people of all ages can form, and yet retain their own lawful customs and habits which are not contrary to the will of God.

How We Got The Bible
Inerrancy
Inerrancy is a term used to explain that the bible is completely true and contains no error in the original autographs. The bible is wholly true in all that it affirms, even Jesus and the writers of the scripture believed in the truthfulness and historical reliability of even the most disputed parts of the Old Testament.

Notice A Few Examples.

While speaking to the Pharisees in the region of Judaea, Jesus confirmed His belief in real existence of an original couple created during the creation week - Matthew 19:4-5, Jesus was referring to Genesis 2:24

Paul regarded the serpent's deception of Eve as a historical event - 2Corinthians 11:3.

Both Jesus and the Apostle Peter believed that Noah was a real person and that the global flood was a historical event - Matthew 24:37-39, 2Peter 2:5,3:6.

Paul attested to the Israelites crossing of the Red Sea, and affirmed his belief in their drinking from a rock - 1Corinthians 10:1-4, Hebrews 11:29 cf, Exodus 14, while Jesus confirmed His belief in the miraculous healing of the Israelites who fixed their eyes on the bronze snake set up by Moses in the desert - John 3:14 cf Numbers 21:4-9.

Jesus regarded the account of Jonah's three days and nights in the belly of a great fish as a historical event - Matthew 12:39-40.

Numerous other examples such as these exist and demonstrate the trustworthiness of the scripture. If Jesus Himself declared in Matthew 5:17-18 that He did come not to destroy the Old Testament book but to fulfil it, then it stands to reason that the bible is God's word without any error.

Is The Bible Really God's Word?
Revelation

There were steps in the process of God's thoughts becoming our written Bibles.

"But I make known to you, brethren, that the gospel which was preached by me is not according to man. For I neither received it from man, nor was I taught it, but it came through the revelation of Jesus Christ." - Galatians 1:11-12 NKJV

"In the time past God spoke to our forefathers through the prophets of many times and in various ways, but in these last days He has spoken to us by His son, whom He appointed heir of all things and through whom He made the universe."- Hebrews 1:1-2

God spoke! God decided to speak to us. If He did not, we would never have known Him. God spoke, He took the initiative to reveal Himself and His ways. God unveiled our minds to the fact that He is God, and He progressively let us know what that meant. No one invented the one true God. He was there and stepped from behind the curtain, and if we are to know more about God, to know Him personally, to know His mind, His ways, He has to speak more clearly, more specifically, and that is what He did. He literally spoke to prophets in the Old Testament in many mysterious ways and to apostles in the New Testament through Jesus. Ultimately He revealed His complete revelation in Jesus who came and taught God's ways and modelled them.

Inspiration

God superintending human writers to compose and record His revelation to mankind. God communication was captured into the writings of the bible by means of "inspiration."- 2Timothy 3:16.

"All scripture is given by inspiration of God, and is profitable for doctrine, for reproof, for correction, for instruction in righteousness."2 Timothy 3:16 NKJV

The bible was written by over 40 different human authors, and you can see how each writer had his own personality and writing style. God did not overshadow them but made sure that each one wrote exactly what He wanted them to say. He inspired them, He spoke to them, His very words became theirs.

"Knowing this first, that no prophecy of scripture is of any private interpretation, for prophecy never came by the will of man, but holy men of God spoke as they were moved by the Holy Spirit."-2 Peter 1:20-21 NKJV

The prophets and the apostles knew when God was speaking. In the Old Testament, the phrase "the word of the Lord " or "God said" occurred 400 times. The New Testament acknowledged the same thing. Paul cites scripture as if it were God speaking. God used the Holy Spirit to make sure that the writers of the scripture recorded exactly what He wanted. There were no errors, there were no contractions, there were no mistakes, and that was not because the writers were meticulous but because God inspired them to write exactly what He wanted them to write.

Canonicity

The term canon comes from the Greek word "Canon" which originally meant "reed." This Greek word meant "rod" or "bar." Since a rod or bar was used for measuring, the word now meant "standard." In grammar, it meant a rule of procedure. In chronology, it meant a table of historical dates, in literature it meant a list of works correctly attributed to a given author.

The English word canon carries two possible connotations:

1. Canon may speak of principles, rules, standards, or norms by which a book is measured before being accepted as part of scripture.

2. Canon may speak of an authoritative list of books accepted as the Holy scripture. The canon is the 66 books recognized as the word of God in the Bible.

Three tests were used to identify which books met the criteria of being divinely inspired:

1. **APOSTOLIC ORIGIN** - by the time of the New Testament writings, the Old Testament had been accepted by the Jews as the authoritative word of God. In the New Testament, the source has to be an apostle or someone closely associated with an apostle. Matthew, John, and Paul had all seen the resurrected Christ. The only non-apostles were Luke, who travelled with Paul, Mark who accompanied Peter, Jude, and James who were Jesus half-brothers.

2. **SOUND IN DOCTRINE** - The writings had to line up with the teachings of Christ, the apostles, and the Old Testament.

3. **RECOGNIZED BY THE EARLY CHURCH** - The early church fathers and councils recognized the 39 Old Testament books and the 27 New Testament books.

God inspired the original manuscripts, which we no longer have because the materials which they wrote on such as papyrus, vellum (animal skins), and parchment only lasted for about 40 years, so the copyist had to keep making new manuscripts to preserve the text from being destroyed. The manuscripts we have today are copies from the original manuscripts, so how do we know that what they copied is accurate?

Transmission

It is the ancient process of accurately copying Hebrew and Greek scriptures for successive generations. The copying of the Bible text was accurate, but it was copied by many scribes. Transmission depended on the scribes using a careful process that God protected. They had no copying machines or duplicating presses, so the manuscripts had to be copied by hand. The Jewish scribes valued the scriptures so much that they counted every letter on every page they copied. Indeed the Israelites viewed the Bible as the word of God, and as a result, not only were they serious about preserving it, but they were also very careful about the transmitting.

There was a whole group of individuals called scribes who were trained for years to copy the Bible. These scribes have a very vigorous set of routines and rules for that process. These rules included:

1. Only master scrolls were used in the duplicating, and a copy was never made from a copy.

2. Scribes were highly and rigorously trained until they were 30years old before they were allowed to begin copying. Being a scribe was a highly esteemed role in the Jewish society.

3. Scribes had to wash ceremonially before working.

4. Anytime the name of God was written, a prayer of sanctification was said.

5. Each letter was counted and compared to the master scroll for accuracy, and the Hebrew word for scribe means "counters" because they counted not only every word but every letter.

6. If a single mistake was made or found, the entire scroll was destroyed.

Given the training of the scribes, the general reverence shown to the word of God, and the stringent rules and procedures used for copying, it was hard to imagine that the Bible could have effectively been altered even if they had desired to do so.

The Septuagint

The Septuagint has been a valuable tool for scholars in determining the accuracy of the Old Testament. The Septuagint was a translation of the Old Testament scriptures from Hebrew to Greek that was done around 280BC, by a team of approximately 70 scholars.

The Dead Sea Scrolls

The single most important event of the last century in verifying the accuracy of our current Old Testament was the discovery of the Dead Sea Scrolls in 1947. Prior to the discovery of the Dead Sea Scrolls, the oldest complete copy of the Old Testament which was discovered was the Masoretic text from approximately 900AD. This gave all kinds of claims that Christians had altered the Old Testament to fit their view of scripture.

That all changed in 1947 when 931 documents were located in a series of caves outside of Jerusalem. Those documents included portions of the Old Testament books. The Old Testament books date to 200BC, well before the birth of Jesus Christ and agree virtually letter for letter with newer copies of the Old Testament like the Masoretic text. Indeed, the degree of accuracy was amazing and deflated arguments that the text had been altered.

The Hebrew nation went to amazing lengths to ensure the accuracy of the transmission of the Old Testament. Furthermore, discoveries like the Dead Sea Scrolls have confirmed the Old Testament we read today is substantially the same as the original.

CHAPTER 2

THE BIBLE TRANSLATION

It is the process of translating the bible from the original Hebrew, Aramaic, and Greek into a modern language. We have many reliable translations in English and other languages. Translation depends on the knowledge and accuracy of the translators and to some degree, upon their interpretive understanding.

Around 400BC, all the books of the Old Testament had been completed. By 300BC the Jews who dwelt in Egypt in the city of Alexandria had begun to translate the Bible from Hebrew to Greek. The five books of Moses were finished around 270BC, and then the remaining books of the Old Testament were translated in the subsequent 150 years. This became the earliest translation of the Hebrew Bible.

According to the letter of Aristeas, this translation was done by 72 scholars, all of whom were experts both Hebrew and Greek. The Greek translation of the Hebrew bible is called the Septuagint, and it is the earliest translation of the Bible.

St. Jerome

In AD 384, the church father, scholar, theologian translated most of the bible into Latin and his commentaries of the gospels. He was born in 347AD in Stridon, Dalmatia.

The Latin translation of the Old Testament from the original Hebrew was finished by AD404. This version was called the Vulgate, which itself is a Latin word meaning "made common."

John Wycliffe

John Wycliffe was born in 1320AD in Yorkshire, England. Had his education at Oxford University. He became an English scholastic philosopher, theologian, biblical translator, reformer, English Priest, and a seminary Professor at the University of Oxford, where his main interest was Biblical studies. As he studied the Holy scriptures and learned Latin and Greek, he started comparing the teachings of the scriptures with the church of his day. Instead of finding harmony, he found only differences with the doctrines and beliefs of the established Catholic Church, and conflicts with practices which had no counterpart in the Biblical manuscripts that Wycliffe was studying.

Wycliffe and his followers called the Lollards could read and understand the bible for themselves, so they started waking up to a secret that had been hidden for centuries, that the church's beliefs, doctrines, and practices were not what the bible taught. People wanted to know what actually the bible said, and read it for themselves because they do not want to be told second-hand by corrupt, lying and powerless priesthood. Their thirst was unquenchable. They hungered and thirst to know the truth of the bible, but the people had a problem, the authority of the Catholic Church was supreme. The Holy scriptures were only available in Latin in the form of vulgate, and only in the form of hand-written manuscripts. Only those like Wycliffe who had the privilege of an education at a university such as Oxford, who were able to understand Latin but the ordinary people had no access to read the bible for themselves, and they could not understand Latin, so they were depending on people like Wycliffe and the Lollards to tell them what the scripture said.

Seeing how ordinary people thirsted for a knowledge of God's word, he became convinced of the need to translate the Latin to which he had access (the Latin Vulgate) into English language spoken by the ordinary people. Only in this way would they be able to read the scriptures for themselves, so a revolutionary idea was conceived into translating the bible from Latin to English. Wycliffe Bible was therefore completed in 1384AD, with further updated versions being done by Wycliffe's assistant John Purvey and others in 1388 AD.

WILLIAM TYNDALE (Father Of The English Bible)

William Tyndale was an English scholar who became a leading figure in the Protestant reformation in the years leading to his execution. Tyndale translation was the first English bible to draw directly from the Hebrew and Greek text. He was born in 1494 in England and died in 1536 at Vilvoorde, near Brussels, Brabant.

Tyndale was educated at the University of Oxford in 1505. He received his Master's Degree in 1515 at the age of 21 and proved to be a gifted linguist. Tyndale associates commented that Tyndale was so skilled in eight languages - Hebrew, Greek, Latin, Spanish, Italian, French, English and German, and whichever he speaks, you would think it was his native tongue.

In 1521, he fell in with a group of humanist scholars and became convinced that the bible should determine the practices and doctrines of the church and that every believer should be able to read the Bible in his own language.

After church authorities in England prevented him from translating the bible there, he went to Germany in 1525 and printed at Cologne. The first copies reached England in 1526. Tyndale then began work on the Old Testament translation, and his version became the basis for most subsequent English translations beginning with the King James Version in 1611. His English translation was the first to use Jehovah as God's name as preferred by English Protestant Reformers, the first English translation to take advantage of the printing press, and the first new English bibles of the Reformation. Eventually, Tyndale was seized in Antwerp in 1535, and held in the castle of Vilvoorde near Brussels. He was tried on a charge of heresy in 1536 and was condemned to be burned to death. Tyndale was strangled to death while tied to the stake, and then his body was burned. His final words spoken at the stake with a fervent zeal, and a loud voice was, "Lord! open the King of England's eyes." Tyndale also told one official who criticised his effort, "if God spares my life, I will see to it that the boy who drives the plowshare knows more of the scriptures than you, Sir!" Within four years, four English translations of the Bible were published in England at the King's behest, including Henry's official Great Bible. All were based on Tyndale's work.

Martin Luther

Martin Luther was a German, born on 10th November 1483, and died 18th February 1546 at the age of 62 years. He was a German professor of theology, composer, monk priest, and a seminal figure in the Protestant Reformation. In 1530 Luther translated the Greek Bible into German.

Myles Coverdale And John Rogers

Myles Coverdale and John Rogers had remained loyal disciples in the last six years of William Tyndale's life, and they carried the English Bible project forward and even accelerated it. Coverdale finished translating the Old Testament, and in 1535 printed the first complete bible in the English language, making use of the Luther's German text and the Latin as sources. Thus, the first complete English Bible was printed on October 4, 1535 and is known as the Coverdale Bible.

Myles Coverdale was born in 1488, educated at Cambridge, became Bishop of Exeter in 1551, but fled during the Reformation. Coverdale spent time living and working in Germany, Switzerland, and Denmark before settling in London as the Rector of St.Magnus.

John Rogers was born in 1505 in Deritend, Birmingham, United Kingdom, and died in 1555. He was educated at Pembroke College, University of Cambridge, Martin Luther University, Halle-Wittenberg. John Rogers guided the development of the Matthew Bible in vernacular English during the reign of Henry VIII and was the first English Protestant martyr under Mary I of England who was determined to restore Roman Catholicism.

In 1555 John Rogers and Thomas Cranmer were both burned at the stake. Queen "bloody" Mary of England went on to burn reformers at the stake in their hundreds for the crime of being a Protestant. This era was known as the

"Mirian Exile," and the refugees fled from England with little hope of ever seeing their home or friends again.

In the 1550's, the church of Geneva, Switzerland was very sympathetic to the reformers refugees and was one of the few havens for the desperate, so many of them met in Geneva, led by Myles Coverdale and John Foxe. There, with the protection of the great theologian John Calvin (author of the most famous theological book ever published, Calvin's Institutes of the Christian Religion) and John Knox, the great Reformer of the Scottish church. The church of Geneva determined to produce a Bible that would educate their families while they continue in exile, so the New Testament was completed in 1557, and the complete Bible was first published in 1560. It became known as the Geneva Bible. The Geneva bible was the first bible to add numbered verses to the chapters so that referencing specific passages would be easier. Every chapter was also accompanied by extensive marginal notes and references. So thorough and complete that the Geneva Bible is also considered the first English study Bible. The Geneva Bible itself retains over 90% of William Tyndale's original English translation, and it is truly the Bible of the Protestant Reformation. With the end of Queen Mary's bloody reign, the reformers could safely return to England. The Anglican Church, now under Queen Elizabeth I reluctantly tolerated the printing and distribution of the Geneva version Bible in England, but the marginal notes which were vehemently against the institutional church of the day did not rest well with the rulers, so in 1568, a version of the Great Bible known as the Bishop's Bible was introduced.

By the 1580s, the Roman Catholic Church saw that it had lost the battle to suppress the will of God, that His holy word is available in English language.

In 1582, the Church of Rome surrendered their fight for Latin only and decided that if the Bible were to be available in English, they would at least have an official Roman Catholic English translation. And so, using the corrupt and inaccurate Latin Vulgate as the only source text, they went on to publish an English Bible with all the distortions and corruptions that Erasmus had revealed and warned of 75 years earlier. Because it was translated at the Roman Catholic College in the city at Rheims, it was known as the Rheims New Testament (also spelled Rhemes).

King James Bible

With the death of Queen Elizabeth I, Prince James the VI of Scotland became King James I of England. The Protestant clergy approached the new king in 1604 and announced their desire for a few translations to replace the Bishop's Bible first printed in 1568. They knew that the Geneva version had won the hearts of the people because of its excellent scholastic, accuracy, and exhaustive commentary. However, they did not want the controversial marginal notes (proclaiming the Pope, an Antichrist, etc.). Essentially, the leaders of the church desired a bible for the people, with scriptural references only for word clarification of cross-references.

Fifty scholars then took into consideration the Tyndale New Testament, the Coverdale Bible, the Matthew Bible, the Great Bible, the Bishop's Bible, the Geneva Bible, and even the Rheims New Testament, and the great work started. From 1605-1606 the scholars engaged in private research, and from 1607-1609 the work was assembled. In 1610 the work went to press, and in 1611 "The King James Bible" came from the printing press.

American Standard Version

In 1901 American Standard Version (ASV) was published. It was widely accepted and embraced by churches throughout America for many decades as the leading modern English version of the Bible.

New American Standard Version Bible - N.A.S.V.

In 1917 the American Standard Version of the Bible was revised and called the New American Standard Version (NASV or NASB). This New American Standard Version is considered by nearly all evangelical Christian scholars translators today, to be the most accurate, word-for-word translation of the original Hebrew and Greek scriptures into the modern English language that has ever been published.

It remains the most popular version among theologians, professors, scholars, and seminary students today. Some, however, have taken issue with it because it is so direct and literal, a translation (focus on accuracy) that it does not flow as easily in conversational English. For this reason, in 1973, the New International Version (NIV) was produced, which was offered as a dynamic equivalent translation into modern English. The New International Version was designed not for word-for-word accuracy, but rather for phrase-for phrase accuracy, and ease of reading even at the junior High school reading level.

New King James Version

In 1982 Thomas Nelson Publishers produced the New King James Version of the Bible (NKJV).

Is The Bible Not A Story Book?

THESE ARE PROPHECIES IN THE OLD TESTAMENT, TIME OF PROPHECY AND ITS FULFILMENT IN THE NEW TESTAMENT TO PROOF THAT THE BIBLE IS INFALLIBLE AND AUTHENTIC.

Prophecy	Date	Fulfilled
He will be born a virgin-Isaiah 7:14	740-680BC	Matthew 1:18-23
He will be the Son of God-Psalm 2:7	1000BC	Matthew 3:17
He will be a descendant of Abraham - Genesis 12:3	22:18, 1400BC	Matt.1:1
The Messiah will be a descendant of Isaac - Genesis 21:12	1400BC	Matt.1:2, Luke 3:34
The Messiah will be a descendant of Jacob - Numbers 24:17	1400BC	Matt.1:2, Luke 3:34
He will be from the tribe of Judah-Gen.49:10	1400BC	Matt.1:2, Lk 3:33
He will be from the family of Jesse - Isaiah 11:1	740-680BC	Matt.1:6, Lk 3:32
The Messiah will be from the house of David - Jeremiah 23:5	627-580BC	Matt.1:1, Lk 3:31
He will be raised up as a prophet like Moses - Deuteronomy 18:15	18, 1400BC	Acts 3:22,7:37
The Messiah will be born in Bethlehem-Micah 5:2	722BC	Matt.2:1
After He was born babies would be killed in Bethlehem-Jeremiah 31:15	627-580BC	Matt.2:16-18
He will be called out of Egypt-Hosea 1:1	720BC	Matt2:15
The Messiah will come from Galilee-Isaiah 9:1-2	740-680BC	Matt.4:13-16
The Spirit of the Lord will be upon Him-Isaiah 61:1	740-680BC	Matt.12:17-18, Lk 4:16-21

He will be proceeded by a messenger-Malachi 3:1	430BC	Matt.11:10
He will do miracles-Isaiah 35:5-6	740-680BC	Matt.11:2-5
Israel King would ride into Jerusalem on a donkey-Zechariah 9:9	470BC	Matt.21:5-9, John 12:14-15
The Messiah would be welcomed with, "blessed is He who comes in the name of the Lord"-Psalm 118:26	1000BC	John 12:13
He will be hated for no reason-Psalm 35:19, 64:4	1000BC	John 15:25
He will be rejected by religious rulers-Psalm 118:22	1000BC	Matt.21:42
He will be rejected by His own brothers-Psalm 69:8	1000BC	John 7:5
He will be betrayed by a friend-Psalm 41:9	1000BC	Matt.10:4
His betrayer will eat bread with Him-Psalm 41:9	1000BC	Mark 14:18, John13:18,26
He would be betrayed for money,30 pieces of silver-Zechariah 11:12	470BC	Matt.26:15
The money would be returned-Zechariah 11:12-13	470BC	Matt.27:3
The money would be thrown in the presence of the Lord-Zechariah 11:13	470BC	Matthew 27:5
The betrayal money would pay for a potter field -Zechariah 11:13	470BC	Matthew 27:7
He will be forsaken by the disciples-13:7	470BC	Matt.26:31,56
He will be silent before His accusers-Isaiah 53:7	740-680BC	Matthew 26:62-63
The Messiah would be mocked - Isaiah 53:3	740-680BC	Matt.27:29
He will be beaten with a rod-Micah 5:1	722	Matt.15:19
He would be spat on the face - Isaiah 50:6	740-680BC	Mark 14:65

The Messiah would be wounded, bruised - Isaiah 53:5	740-680BC	Matt.27:30, Lk 22:63
The Messiah would be scourged on the back - Isaiah 50:6, 53:5	740-680BC	John 19:1
His hands and feet would be pierced - Psalm 22:16	1000BC	Jn 20:25
His garment would be divided - Psalm 22:18	1000BC	John 19:23
They would cast lots for His clothing - Psalm 22:16	1000BC	Jn 19:24
The Messiah would die with criminals - Isaiah 52:12	740-680BC	Mark 15:28, Luke 22:37
Those watching the crucifixion would mock Him for not saving Himself - Psalm 22:8	1000BC	Matt.27:41-43
Those watching Him at the crucifixion would wag their heads - Psalm 22:7, 109:25	1000BC	Mk 15:29, 27:39
He would pray for those crucifying Him - Isaiah 53:12	740-680BC	Lk 23:34
He would be given vinegar to drink - Psalm 69:21	1000BC	Matt.27:34
"Why hast thou forsaken me?" - Psalm 22:11	1000BC	Matt.27:46
"Unto thy hands, I commit my Spirit" - Psalm 31:5	1000BC	Lk 23:46
His side would be pierced - Zechariah 12:10	470BC	Jn 19:34,37
None of the Messiah's bone would be broken - Psalm 34:20	1000BC	Jn 19:32-36
He would be buried in a rich man's tomb - Isaiah 53:9	740-680BC	Matt.27:57-60
He would descend into hell - Psalm 16:10, 49:15	1000BC	Acts 2:27, 31, Ephesians 4:9
The Messiah would be resurrected from the dead - Psalm 16:10, 30:3	1000BC	Acts 2:31, 13:33-35

Through His resurrection, He would swallow up death in victory - Isaiah 25:8	740-680BC	1 Corinthians 15:54
He would ascend to heaven - Psalm 68:18	1000BC	Acts 1:9, Ephesians 4:8-10
He would be seated at the right hand of the Father in heaven -Psalm 110:1	1000BC	Acts 2:34-35, Colossians 3:1
He would be a priest according to the order of Melchizedek - Psalm 110:4	1000BC	Hebrew 5:6,10,6:20
The Messiah would be a light to the entire world including non-Jews - Isaiah 42:6,49:6	740-680BC	Lk 2:32, Acts 13:47,26:23

Jesus fulfilled more than 300 prophecies in the Bible. The evidence is so compelling that it should convince you beyond any reasonable doubt. God left His fingerprint on these prophecies so that you could figure out that He is real and the Bible is true.

When Was The Bible Written?

GENESIS - 1445BC, EXODUS - 1445BC, LEVITICUS - 1445BC

NUMBERS - 1405BC, DEUTERONOMY - 1405BC, JOSHUA - 1405-1385BC

JUDGES - 1043BC, RUTH - 1000BC, 1&2 SAMUEL 1000-900BC,

1&2 KINGS - 561-538BC, 1&2 CHRONICLES - 538-333BC, EZRA - 538-515BC,

NEHEMIAH - 425BC, ESTHER - 475BC, JOB - lived in the Patriarchal times, probably 2100-900BC, PSALMS - 1450-500BC, PROVERBS - 950BC, ECCLESIASTES - 931BC, SONG OF SOLOMON - 960BC, ISAIAH - 740-680BC, JEREMIAH - 627-580BC, LAMENTATIONS - 586BC, EZEKIEL - 570BC

DANIEL - 536BC, HOSEA - 570, JOEL - 830BC, AMOS - 760BC

OBADIAH - 845BC, JONAH - 780BC, MICAH - 735-722BC, NAHUM - 661-612BC, HABAKKUK-609BC, ZEPHANIAH - 635BC, HAGGAI - 520BC, ZECHARIAH - 520-470BC, MALACHI - 430BC.

MATTHEW - 50AD, MARK - 50AD, LUKE - 60-61AD, JOHN - 80-90AD

ACTS - 63AD, ROMANS - 56AD, 1&2 CORINTHIANS - 54-56AD,

GALATIANS - 48AD, EPHESIANS - 61AD, PHILIPPIANS - 62AD,

COLOSSIANS - 62AD, 1&2 THESSALONIANS - 51AD, 1TIMOTHY - 62AD,

2TIMOTHY - 64AD, TITUS - 63AD, PHILEMON - 61AD, HEBREWS - 65AD,

JAMES - 45AD, 1 Peter - 65AD, 2 Peter - 67AD, 1JOHN - 65AD

2JOHN - 90AD, 3JOHN - 90AD, JUDE - 70AD, REVELATION - 95AD.

PART TWO

CHAPTER 3

WHO IS JESUS?

The controversy surrounding the deity of Jesus Christ has been a hot debate for a very long time, but the truth of the matter is revealed in the Bible."Iesous" the Greek word for Jesus meaning Jehovah is salvation or Saviour.

The world knows that 2000 years ago, a man named Jesus (our Lord) arose from the town of Nazareth, Israel. He travelled around the region and gained a large following. After a few years, the religious leaders in Jerusalem falsely accused Him of crimes and handed Him to the Roman authorities to be crucified by nailing Him to the cross, but on the third day, He rose from the dead. His disciples preached in His name with signs and wonders following, and more followers were added to His church daily, which has become the Christianity of today.

These are facts upon which even the greatest sceptic will agree, but there is so much more about Jesus than that. Where He came from, what He did on earth, what He can do for us now, are all revealed in the Bible. The Bible contains the only record of Jesus and was written by the generation of the people who heard Him and saw His deeds. Who really is Jesus then?

He is God, begotten from the substance of the Father before all ages, and He is man, born from the substance of His mother in His age. Perfect God and perfect man, composed of a rational soul and human flesh. He is equal to the Father with respect to His divinity, less than the Father with respect to His humanity.

Although He is God and man, He is not two but one Christ. For as the rational soul and flesh is one man, so God and man is one Christ. He suffered for our salvation, descended into hell, rose again the third day from the dead, ascended into heaven, and is seated at the right hand of the Father, God Almighty, from whence He will come and judge the living and the dead. At His coming, all people will rise again with their new bodies and give an account concerning their own deeds. Christians believe, teach and confess that Jesus Christ is our Saviour and Lord, and that through faith in Him, we receive forgiveness of sins, salvation and eternal life. Jesus alone has been ordained to be the mediator and propitiation through whom the Father is reconciled. Jesus Christ is the only way to heaven and that all who die without faith in Him are eventually damned.

Who Is Jesus Christ?

He is God, who 2000 years ago, walked among men. "Behold, the virgin shall be with a child, and bear a son, and they shall call His name Immanuel, which is translated, God with us." **Matthew 1:23**

Who Is This Jesus?

"Then He said to them, These are the words which I spoke to you while I was still with you, that all things must be fulfilled which were written in the law of Moses and the prophets and the psalms concerning Me."

— Luke 24:44

Jesus is God. He is the word of God made flesh. Jesus is God, by Him and through Him, all things were created. The God who once upon a time walked, dinned, and talked with men but the sad news was that man did not recognise Him.

In the beginning was the word, and the word was with God, and the word was God. He was in the beginning with God. All things were made through Him, and without Him nothing was made that was made." John 1:1-3. verse 14 "And the word became flesh and dwelt among us, and we beheld His glory, the glory as of the only begotten of the Father, full of grace and truth."

"For by Him all things were created that are in heaven and that are on earth, visible and invisible, whether thrones or dominions or principalities or powers. All things were created through Him and for Him. And He is before all things, and in Him all things consist."

— **Colossians 1:16-17.**

Jesus Christ (the word made flesh) is the creator of everything, visible and invisible. That is things we can see with our naked eyes and vice versa, things in heaven and on earth, whether thrones, dominions, principalities or powers, all things were created by Him (Jesus, the word of God made flesh), and they are for Him, including you and I.

In **Matthew 11:28**, Jesus made a profound statement, *"come to Me, all you who labour and are heavy laden, and I will give you rest."* The question is, can Jesus give us rest as He has said? Yes He can! The reason is, He created everything, He has the power to fix that which is wrong. For if the Samsung company can fix that faulty Samsung phone because they manufactured it, then Jesus the creator of all things can fix everything, including that which is wrong in your life.

WHO IS JESUS?

> *"He is the image of the invisible God, the firstborn over all creation."*
>
> — **Colossians 1:15**

Jesus Christ is God in human form or flesh. He existed before everything was created. He is the founder and supreme Head of the church. He is the Author and Giver of everything, we should, therefore, depend on Him for the supply of all things. "And you are complete in Him, who is the head of all principality and power." Colossians 2:10.

When we have Christ, we have everything, including eternal life and total victory in this life because He is the Highest Ruler with authority over every other power. At the mentioning of His name, demons tremble. His presence disorganises and puts the kingdom of darkness into submission. Satan himself cannot operate unless permission is given from the Highest power according to Job 1:12. The angel told Mary when the power of the Highest overshadow you all impossibilities will become possible.

> *"Then He said to them, These are the words which I spoke to you while I was still with you, that all things must be fulfilled which were written in the law of Moses, and the prophets and the psalms concerning Me."*
>
> — **Luke 24:44.**

Jesus is the word of God (the Bible) made flesh, from Genesis to Revelation. Let us consider the above scripture verse. Jesus categorically made it plain to His disciples that starting from the law of Moses, that is from Genesis to Deuteronomy (Torah) were about Him. Then the prophets, and that is from the book of Joshua to Malachi, were also about Him. We then have the psalms, from Job to Song of Solomon, were also about Him. We, therefore, conclude from the above scripture that the Bible is about Jesus, the word of the living God.

Jesus is pictured or prophesied about in each of the 66 books, as well as in countless types of different characters in the Bible.

In Genesis, Jesus is pictured as the seed of the woman - **Genesis.3:15.**

In Exodus, Jesus is pictured as the Passover lamb - **Exodus.12, John 1:29-36**.

In Leviticus, He is the High **Priest - Leveticus.1-7.**

In Numbers, He is the pillar of cloud by day and fire by night - **Numbers 9:16**

In Deuteronomy, He is the prophet like unto Moses - **Deut.18:15-19.**

In Joshua, He is the captain of our salvation - **Joshua 5:13-15.**

In Judges, He is the judge and the lawgiver - **Judges 2:11-15.**

In Ruth, He is the Kingsman Redeemer - **Ruth 4:12-17.**

In 1&2 Samuel He is the prophet of the Lord - 1Samuel.2:10, 2 Samuel.7:12-16.

In 1&2 Kings, He is the Reigning King — 1 Kings 2:33,45.

In 1&2 Chronicles, He is the glorious Temple - 1 Chronicles.5:2.

In Ezra, He is the Faithful Scribe - Ezra 4.

In Nehemiah, He is the builder of the broken wall — Nehemiah 2:20.

In Esther, He is our Mordecai - **Esther 2:10, 8:3.**

In Job, He is the Dayspring from on high **- Job 38:12**.

In Psalms, He is the good Shepherd **- Psalm 2:7, 16:8-10, 22:6-8.**

In Proverbs and Ecclesiastes, He is the wisdom of God **- Proverbs. 8:22-23, 30:4**.

In Isaiah, He is the suffering servant **- Isaiah 7:14, Isaiah 9:6.**

In Jeremiah and Lamentations, He is the weeping prophet **- Jeremiah .23:6, 23:5.**

In Ezekiel, He is the Son of man **- Ezekiel 34:23-24.**

In Daniel, He is the Son of man coming in the cloud of heaven **- Daniel.7:13-14**.

In Hosea, He is the Bridegroom **- Hosea 3.**

In Joel, He is the Baptiser of the Holy Spirit **- Joel 2:28-32.**

In Amos, He is the burden-bearer **- Amos 8:9.**

In Obadiah, He is the mighty Saviour. **Obadiah 1:1-16.**

In Jonah, He is the forgiving God **- Jonah 1:17.**

In Micah, He is the messenger with beautiful feet **- Micah 5:2.**

In Nahum, He is the avenger of God's elect. - **Nahum 1:3**.

In Habakkuk, He is the great evangelist crying for revival - **Habakuk.3:3**.

In Zephaniah, He is the restorer of the remnant - **Zephaniah 3:9-20**.

In Haggai, He is the cleansing fountain - **Haggai 2:6-9**.

In Zechariah, He is the pierced Son - **Zechariah 6:12-13, 9:9**.

In Malachi, He is the Sun of Righteousness - **Malachi.4:2**.

In Matthew, He is the Messiah - **Matthew.1:1, 2:2, 2:5**.

In Mark, He is the miracle worker - **Mark.1:24, 15:32**.

In Luke, He is the Son of man - **Luke.1:69, 2:25**.

In John, He is the Son of God - **John 1:14,18**.

In Acts, He is the ascended Lord - **Acts 3:15**.

In Romans, He is the Justifier - **Romans.9:33, 11:26, 14:9**.

In 1&2 Corinthians, He is the last Adam - **1Corinthians.15:45**.

In Galatians, He is the one who sets us free - **Galatians.1:3**.

In Ephesians, He is the Christ of riches - **Ephesians.1:22, 2:20**.

In Philippians, He is the God who meets our every need - **Philipians.2:19**.

In Colossians, He is the fullness of the Godhead - **Colossians.1:15**.

In 1&2 Thessalonians, He is the soon coming King - **2Thessalonians.3:16**.

In 1&2 Timothy He is the mediator between God and man - 1Timothy.1:17, 2:5.

In Titus, He is the blessed Hope - **Titus 2:13.**

In Philemon, He is the friend closer than a brother - **Philemon 3.**

In Hebrews, He is the Blood that washes away our sins - **Hebrew.1:2, 2:17, 12:2.**

In James, He is the Great Physician - **James.2:1, 5:9.**

In 1&2 Peter, He is the Chief Shepherd - **1Peter2:4, 5:4.**

In 1, 2 &3 John, He is the Everlasting Love - **1John 1:2, 2:1.**

In Jude, He is the God our Saviour - **Jude 2:5.**

In Revelation, He is the King of kings and Lord of lords - **Revelation.1:17, 5:5, 19:13, 22:13, 22:16.**

CHAPTER 4

JESUS IN THE OLD TESTAMENT

I delivered a message on prayer and taught the congregation on how Jesus was in constant communion with the Father in prayer, as the scripture teaches. Jesus will go to the mountain or a solitary place and pray all night because He (The Word) needed to tap power from heaven to effect change in the lives of the people through prayer. I, therefore, admonished the congregation to emulate the master and desist from the so-called "directions," which some Christians receive from some men of God which do not have any biblical foundation or support.

Two days after the message, a woman came to narrate to me how she won a lottery through some numbers she got by revelation. According to this woman she fasted for three days, and on the third day a spirit (which I know was not the Holy Spirit) directed her to a cement block, and on it were written two numbers which the spirit told her to go and try her luck on lottery, which she won outrightly. According to this woman, she was desperately in need of money for her wedding hence the fasting.

After she had finished narrating her story, I asked if she still plays the game of lotto, the reply was no! But she lied. I sat her down for almost an hour and explained things to her by the word of God. In the first place, I told her that there is nothing like chance or gambling with God, for God has already blessed every believer spiritually and physically, but these blessings are in the spirit. What the Christian has to do is to tap into the spirit and release these things into the physical.

Secondly, our financial prosperity is hidden in our gifts (talents) which God has given to us, we need to identify and polish them. God does not prosper His children through chance, luck or gambling, I told her. The fact that you fasted for three days does not mean that the voice you heard was automatically the voice of God. The first person Jesus encountered after His forty days and nights fasting was the devil. Thank God at the end of the meeting, this woman was enlightened and understood biblical principles to the glory of God.

There was this young pastor I met who has a calling in the ministry with a unique gift upon his life, but the love for money has made him moved away from the truth. He loves to do God's work but so desperate for money to the extent that he will do everything in the name of ministry to get money. He has counselling days on which he receives clients and gives them directions.

He told a brother who needed a United States visa to bath with a special soap which he bought from a special shop for a week. The brother was to put a brand-new kitchen knife in a Bible and sleep on it for three days, not only that; he was also directed to put an olive oil and wine in a horn and bury them. Some of the materials he uses as directions for his clients are special expensive soaps, knives, different colours of oil, horns, wine and many more. Sometimes this pastor gets his directions from the internet, and the damage here is that peoples' minds are shifted from God's Principles and processes to magic. Now because they rely on special revelations and directions, the church service becomes a mere formality to them, they go to church no doubt, but their hearts and minds are not in the church service. The pastor is selling lies, deceit, and death to many but because of desperations, ignorance, vain glory, and greed men do not care.

A brother who joined our church recently also narrated his agony to me, and it was terrible. He saw on the television one of these prophets and was deceived by their signs and deceiving wonders, and before he could say "Jack," all his money was gone. This man who has now been saved needed an entry visa to Netherlands, so he approached the prophet and was directed to do so many weird things besides that, he was asked to pay a huge sum of money, but unfortunately, all amounted to nothing, the poor brother told me. His business was on the verge of collapsing due to the huge sum of money that he gave to the prophet. My people are deceived for lack of knowledge the scripture says.

The false prophets have made people to believe that the blood of Jesus is not enough to save and deliver mankind hence the practices of Judaism, magic, and astrology in Christendom. The practices that were going on in Colossae church is here with us, and it is not helping the body of Christ. We need the 'Pauls' to speak against some of these heresies, and at this moment knowledge, wisdom, and understanding are urgently needed in our churches to expose the kingdom of darkness and enlighten the believer. For I have personally seen some churches with great number of people attending church service but without bibles, and the gospel also not being preached there, the least said about altar call, the better. After watching them on television and YouTube, the only thing I do ask is that, are these people glorifying God? Are the leaders leading these great number of people to Christ? Are they preparing themselves for heaven? Let me take this opportunity to advise anyone who gets a copy of this book to read, that power to bring about change in our lives is not in objects. Power is not with creation but the creator. Power is not in that Samsung television set but the manufacturer of that TV set. When that product made or manufactured is faulty, it will only take the manufacturer to fix it. The power we need to effect change in our lives is in Jesus, the creator, and giver of everything. He is the Highest Ruler with authority over every other power. Power is not in rods, knives, neither is it in special objects and places. In this last days, Jesus Christ fulfils everything.

Scriptures teach clearly how Jesus went about His successful ministry on earth. In the night, the scripture says He will go to the mountain or a solitary place and pray all-night. Pray for what? For power to effect change, power to bring smiles into peoples' lives. If the word that created everything went unto His knees and prayed for power, then we have to even pray the more. As one study the word he or she will realise that during the day the master teaches the multitude, heal the sick and work miracles, but in the evenings, He goes to the mountains and prays. It was prayer, prayer and prayer and nothing else. It was communicating with the Father and tapping power to bring smiles into peoples' faces. If we want to break barriers, tear down Jericho walls, and move mountains, then we need to spend more time with the Father. We need to stir up the power within us, call the Holy Spirit to battle. It is about time we get enlightened and know how things work in the Christendom. It is about time to deal with ignorance and the kingdom of darkness so that we can become what God wants us to be.

"God, who at various times and in various ways spoke in time past to the fathers by the prophets, has in these last days spoken to us by His Son, whom He has appointed heir of all things, through whom also He made the worlds."

— Hebrews 1:1-2

As I said earlier, God's power is not in objects, the power of God is not found in an ark as it used to be, neither could God's power be found in rods or oils. The oil in the New Testament is a symbol of the Holy Spirit like a dove. The Holy Spirit who is the third person in the Trinity, cannot stay in oils and doves; it is not possible, for the power of God could only be found in the gospel of Jesus Christ. Apostle Paul said it clearly in Romans 1:16, "For I am not ashamed of the gospel of Christ, for it is the power of God to salvation for everyone who believes, for the Jews first and also the Greek." As Christians lift up holy hands and pray according to God's word, we stir up the Holy Spirit who is already inside us into battle. The Old Testament way of worship has given way to the law of the spirit of life in Christ Jesus; that is, we do not worship God by observing the law of Moses, such that animal sacrifices are performed, but we worship God in the spirit and in truth. Hebrews chapters 8,9 and 10 teach us that the Old Testament Jewish worship gave a dim (shadow) of the good things Christ would do for us. The law, the animal sacrifices, the symbols were shadows indicating that the real was on the way coming which is Christ.

In 2007 I was invited to speak at a conference in Nairobi, Kenya. It was a week destiny conference which brought people from within and around Kenya. During the conference a benevolent family invited me for a dinner, so I went with the host pastor. When we got there, the food was not ready, and as we were waiting for the food, Martin, the last child of this family who was about eight years of age brought his examination papers just to show them to me. Martin was very good in class as I glanced through the papers, but there was one question Martin got it wrong. The question went like this: Jesus Christ was — to His parents.

(a) bad (b) obedient (c) disobedient.

Martin unknowingly ticked (a) meaning, Jesus Christ was "bad" to His parents, so the teacher marked him wrong. I asked Martin why he got that particular question wrong, and his response was," Bishop, I did not understand the question." "But now you understand right," I asked Martin and he responded yes! Precious one, let us learn something here. The scripture says wisdom is a principal thing, and in all our getting we should get understanding. Martin got the question wrong because he did not understand the question. Suppose he got all the questions wrong; the teacher would have told him to repeat the class. Whenever we get things done wrongly, we suffer, and if we become ignorant about the scriptures, we will struggle. Jesus in Matthew 22:29, told the Pharisees, you are in error because you do not know the scriptures nor the power of God. One of the primary weapons of the devil is ignorance, he tries hard to keep man away from knowing the truth, and once the truth is not known mistakes are inevitable. The purpose of this book is to help the reader understand that Jesus is the answer to every question one can think of. Jesus is the fulfilment of the Old Testament law, the various feast, and the animal sacrifices. The old Jewish law was a foreshadow that Jesus who is the reality was coming, and He has come, we then look to Jesus who is the author and finisher of our faith.

"Then I fell down at his feet to worship him, but he said, no! Don't! For I am a servant of God just as you are, and as your Christian brother are, who testify of your faith in Jesus. The purpose of all prophecy and all I have shown you is to tell about Jesus."

— Revelation 19:10, TLB

The purpose of all the visions, prophecies, crusades, conferences, 40, 50, 100 days fasting, etc. is to tell people about Jesus, (winning souls for Jesus) else work done is zero. That is the meaning of Revelation 19:10.

"Then He said to them, these are the words which I spoke to you while I was still with you, that all things must be fulfilled which were written in the law of Moses, and the prophets and the Psalms concerning Me."

— Luke 24:44.

The Bible from Genesis to Revelation is about Jesus. Let us do a little typology here. Do not be scared of the word typology, for it is just the study of types and antitypes in the Bible, and it will help us to understand the bible better and start believing right, and once we believe right, we will act right, and get the right results.

It is said that a picture is worth a thousand words. The entire Bible speaks about Jesus, but the Old Testament is about, types, shadows, pictures and prophecies of Jesus. There are hundreds, even thousands of years between the types, shadows, pictures, and prophecies of Jesus and when Jesus lived His life on earth. Not only do these shows how wonderful and divinely inspired the Bible is, the pictures of Jesus in the Old Testament help show us more about this wonderful person.

Typology

Typology is simply the study of types and antitypes in the Bible. Typology of the Old Testament is the picture language in which the doctrines of the New Testament, such as the atonement are figured. An example is the "brazen serpent" and "the cross" Numbers 21:8-9, John 3:14-15.

"And as Moses lifted up the serpent in the wilderness, even so must the Son of man be lifted up. "That whoever believes in Him should not perish but have eternal life."

— John 3:14-15.

1 Corinthians 10:1-11, in verse 11, "Now all these things happened unto them as examples, and they were written for our admonition, upon whom the ends of the ages have come."

Apostle Paul was speaking of the children of Israel, and the things that happened to them from the time of their Egyptian bondage until they reached the promised land. So, we see that while the Old Testament is a record of the history of the children of Israel, the events of that history are more than mere events, they are the typical plan of salvation. The writer of Hebrews tells us that the 'types' are but shadows of good things to come, and not the very image of the thing - Hebrews 10:1. That is, the Old Testament 'types' are but 'shadows.' But there cannot be a shadow without some real thing to make it. And a shadow is not the very image of the thing, for a shadow is out of proportion, and is an imperfect representation of the thing it reveals. So the Old Testament Types are Shadows in the sense that they are not the real thing and are but imperfect revelation of it.

Types

I believe the question in your mind would be, what is type?

Let us see how William G. Morehead (The Int'l. Standard Bible Encyclopaedia) defines it.

" Types are pictures, objects - lessons by which God taught His people concerning His grace and saving power. The Mosaic system was a sort of kindergarten in which God's people were trained in divine things, by which also they were led to look for better things to come."

"Types' are Old Testament institutions, events, persons, objects and ceremonies which has reality and purpose in Biblical history, but which also by divine designs foreshadows something yet to be revealed."

The English word 'type' is translated from the Greek word 'Tupos' which literally means the mark or impression made on a soft substance by a blow. It is derived from the verb "to strike" and has a wide range of meanings in the New Testament. For example, it is used in this literal way for the work of the nails in the hands of our Lord Jesus - John 20:25.

The New Testament also used the word 'antitupos' in Greek, meaning 'antitypes' in which the types in the Old Testament foreshadows the antitypes in the New Testament. In this way, the lifted brazen serpent in Numbers 21:8-9 on the cross in the wilderness prefigured the Son of man crucifixion on the cross of Calvary. In this way, the lifted brazen serpent was the 'type' (shadow, picture) "tupos", the Son of man, Jesus crucifixion on the cross of Calvary was the antitype (antitupos) the reality. The Old Testament institutions, ceremonies, persons and events were types (tupos) pictures, shadows and powerless to save the soul of men, they were devised as types of Christ (antitypes).

For example the Tabernacle, which typified the place and the manner in which God met with His people and dealt with their sins, was a type of the incarnate Christ and His ministry for men.

The priesthood typified the one and only perfect priest, the Lord Jesus Christ. The offerings, objects, feasts, and ceremonies all typified things having to do with redemption through the Messiah and the life of the redeemed. The Old Testament people were a type of the New Testament people of faith.

CHAPTER 5

JESUS IN THE TABERNACLE

At a point in Israel's history, when the law was given, God instructed Moses to build something known as the tabernacle. Basically, every aspect of this tabernacle and its incredible design points to Christ in one form or another. He is central, hence the need to study it to rightly divide the word of truth.

Who was the originator of the tabernacle?

What were the reasons for its construction and what did God desire to teach us?.

What materials was it constructed from, and what do they symbolically represent?

What did the three areas of the tabernacle represent concerning Jesus, salvation and the different dispensation?

"Then the Lord spoke to Moses, saying, tell the sons of Israel to raise a contribution for Me, from every man whose heart moves him you shall raise My contribution. And this is the offering which you shall take from them: gold, silver, and bronze, blue, purple and scarlet thread, fine linen, and goat hair, ram skins dyed red, badger skins, and acacia wood, oil for the light, and spices for the anointing oil and for the sweet incense: Onyx stones, and stones to be set in the ephod and in the breastplate. And let them make Me a sanctuary, that I may dwell among them. According to all that I show you, that is, the pattern of the tabernacle and the pattern of all its furnishings, just so you shall make it."- Exodus 25:1-9.

God decided that there should be a tabernacle and it's construction had to be exact to the pattern that God would give to Moses. If God said an item was 100 cubits long, then 100 cubits it was. Why did God want a tabernacle constructed and why did it have to be so exact to His specification? And what was God teaching Israel, and then what is He trying to teach you and I now?

What The Tabernacle Teaches

There are some key "truths" contained within the tabernacle, these truths are interwoven into its size, its materials, and the objects it contains.

Jesus

First and foremost, the tabernacle is a picture and type of that which takes the place of pre-eminence in the Bible, and that is the person of Christ Jesus, the Son of the living God. He is the true fulfilment of this structure. As the amplified Bible brings out "And the word (Christ) became flesh (human incarnate) and tabernacled (fixed His tent of flesh, lived a while) among us, and we (actually) saw His glory (His honour, His majesty), such glorying as an only begotten Son receives from His Father, full of grace (favour, loving kindness) and truth." John 1:14.

The Presence And The Holiness Of God

We read above that God said that the tabernacle was to be constructed so that God may dwell among them. God wanted to be in the midst of His people, but His people are sinful, so how could a Holy God dwell among His people? The tabernacle taught God's desire for fellowship along with His pure holiness.

The Plan Of Salvation

The earthly tabernacle pictures salvation and the steps necessary for those who want to be saved. Jesus had to fulfil His role as the High Priest of the New Covenant entering into the heavenly tabernacle as in the book of Hebrews 9:11-12,24.

The Dispensation And Ages In The Plan Of God

The tabernacle teaches about God's plan concerning the different ages or dispensations in His dealings with man. Each of the three distinct areas (outer court, the Holy Place, and the Holy of Holies) represents a different dispensation, and the objects found within each are true to that age.

Clues In The Colours And Materials

Let us have a look at the materials that God specifically said had to be used in its construction. Everything, whether it was the curtains, the gate, the altar, the lampstand or the Ark of the covenant itself, were constructed from the materials mentioned by God. Therefore, it is worth examining these, for we shall see them and again.

ITEM, SYMBOLIC, MEANING, REFERENCES

Gold - Deity - 1Corinthians.3:12, Revelation.21:18-21

Silver - Redemption Exodus.36:24,30:15, 36:24

Brass/Bronze - Judgement Exo.27:2,Number.21:9,Rev.1:5

Blue - Heaven/Heavenly Nature Exodus.25:4,26:31,28:31

Purple - Kingly/Royalty Jn.19:2, Revelation.17:4

Scarlet - Blood Sacrifice/Jesus suffering Leviticus 14:4, Jos 2:18, Isa.1:8

Fine Linen - Righteousness Leviticus 6:10,Rev 19:8

Goats/Rams Hair - Atonement Genesis.15:9, Exo.12:5

Acacia Wood - Jesus Humanity Exodus.26:15, Isa.53:2

Oil - Holy Spirit- Leviticus 14:16, Ps.47:7

The Three Areas And Meanings Of The Tabernacle

1. The Outer Court - Mosaic Law -1500 cubits - Jesus as the WAY — Justification.

2. The Holy Place - Grace (church age) 2000 cubits - the TRUTH — Sanctification.

3. The Holy of Holies - Messianic Kingdom - 1000 cubits — LIFE — Glorification.

Each of these areas represents an age or dispensation of God's dealing with mankind. This is evident in the objects constructed and the materials used.

The Outer Court

The outer court contained the brazen altar and the laver. The focus was on sacrifice, judgement, and cleansing and represents the age of the law. The area of the fence surrounding the outer court was 1500 cubits squared just as the period of the time that the law was in force. Everything in the outer court was constructed in bronze symbolising judgement, and this is what the law did. It pronounced you guilty and that is judgement, and therefore a blood sacrifice was required. But it is also pointed to Jesus as the way of salvation and the need for justification.

The Holy Place

The second area of the Holy Place was different because it represents the church age. Its area confirms this as it was a room of 20x10x10 cubits (representing the 2000 years of the church age). Only the priests could come within this area and with cleansing at the laver. But this area contained no item made of bronze (judgement) like the outer court did. It contained the showbread (Christ the bread of life), the lampstand (Christ the light of the world), and the altar of incense (Christ our intercessor). It was made from gold, silver, and wood representing the deity, redemption, and the humanity of Christ. It pictures Jesus as the 'truth,' and in terms of salvation, it represents our need of sanctification as we walk in this life with Christ as our life and bread.

The Holy Of Holies

This contained the Ark of the covenant. Only the High Priest could enter here and only once a year, which is the day of atonement and be in the presence of God Himself. This area represents the coming Kingdom age, where God shall dwell among His people once again in visible form. In terms of the aspect of the believer's salvation, it represents our glorification. This special area of the tabernacle contained the very real presence and power of God, and if we are to know Jesus today as the life (and not just the way) then we too, as priest of the new covenant, need to come into His very presence in the new way opened to us.

Only One Way - Exodus 27:9-19

The first thing that we see was that the tabernacle outer court was enclosed by a fence. There was only one way into the court, and this was through an entrance on the east side. This entrance itself is a picture (type) of the Lord Jesus. He is the door. In this way, the 'door' is the type and Jesus is the antitype. Jesus is the gate. He is the only way unto salvation. As Jesus said "I am the gate, whoever enters through Me will be saved. He will come in and go out, and will find pasture "- John 10:9.

Now put yourself in the place of someone approaching this entrance. As you approach this gate you would have first noticed the colours on the curtain. Blue, purple and scarlet threads made up the fine linen curtain entrance. These colours would remind you that you were entering that which was heavenly and it involved royalty, and the scarlet would have reminded you that this was also a place of sacrifice and blood. As you thought of fine linen, you would have been reminded that this was a place of complete righteousness. By about now, you would be holding your breath somehow, and you have only just approached the gate. But as you go through that gate, a solemn site would confront you, for directly in your way would be the brazen altar with its sacrifice and perpetual fire.

The Brazen Altar

The first solemn object seen at the outer court is the brazen altar. The Altar has four horns in each corner where the sacrificial animal was bound and killed by the priests. These sacrifices went on daily, and the command from God was that the fire for this altar was never to go out. Something else stood out as you look around, everything was made from bronze. The altar itself was made from acacia wood but was completely covered in bronze. All the utensils were bronze, even the wooden poles used to carry the altar were covered with bronze. This entire spoke of judgement.

This altar, of course, has its fulfilment on the cross, and it was the picture of the sacrifice for sin that Jesus accomplished at Calvary. At the brazen altar, the animals had to be tied down to the four horns for they did not want to die, but Jesus went willingly to the cross saying "greater love has no man than he lays down his life for his friends."Jesus was the final sacrifice because He took all the judgement of God. Anyone who is in Christ is forever saved.

Place Of Refuge

Praise God that this altar was also a place of refuge. Many in Israel's history fled to the altar when they thought they might die and grabbed hold of the horns. An example is recorded for us in 1Kings1:50. When Adonijah, David's son, had wrongfully tried to exalt himself as king. So, while the altar is a place of judgement and sacrifice, it is also a place of refuge. By grabbing the altar, Adonijah was saying in effect, "I deserve to die for my sin, I deserve to be judged, I associate myself with these that are sacrificed on this altar in the hope that I may find mercy and have my sin forgiven." And mercy was found for Adonijah. Likewise, for mankind, today God is asking the sinner to come to this altar (altar call), the cross, and associate themselves with the sacrifice that was made on their behalf 2000 years ago. We grab hold of the horns so to speak, as we see that Christ was our substitute that day. He took the place that we deserve so that we can now find mercy and eternal life through the payment with His life that He made for our sins.

The Bronze Laver - (Exodus 30:17-21, Exo.38:8)

As you move a little forward from the bronze altar, you have the bronze laver. This was for the priest to wash from before ministering at the Holy Place. As you peer into the laver, you are faced with yourself. The laver was made from the polished bronze that the women used for their mirrors - Exodus 38:8.

This laver of bronze symbolises Christ, our cleanser, who cleanses us from our defilement. It denotes spiritual renewal. We have daily cleansing from defilement of life, and it is accessible only through our Priest. We are continually cleansed by Christ through the Spirit and the word - John 15:3, Eph 5:25-27, 1John 1:6-9.

We look at the outer court that contained the brazen altar, and the brazen laver. It was bronze, bronze, bronze wherever we looked. It is time to leave the outer court behind, with its emphasis on judgement and sacrifice, and move into the holy place. There we shall see no more bronze but gold and acacia wood. The three objects in this room will give us a greater insight into different aspects of the Lord Jesus Christ. They shall also show us what is required to make the next step from salvation to fellowship with Christ. Let us begin with the first object.

The Table Of Showbread - Exo.25:23-30

As you are into the Holy Place, the first article that you see is the table of showbread. This table has twelve loaves of bread on it, each representing the twelve tribes of Israel. Leviticus 24:5-9 tells us that the showbread was made of fine flour and set on the table, sprinkled lightly with frankincense. The bread could be eaten by the priests only and replaced weekly. This table being made of acacia wood and overlaid with gold represents the person of Christ. Again emphasising His humanity of life. You will remember John 6:32-35, what Jesus said: "I tell you the truth, it is not Moses who has given you the bread from heaven."

The One Amazing Lamp-Exo.25:31-40.

We read that the lampstand is made out of pure gold. There is no acacia wood or any other material used here, just pure gold. So straight away, we see that we are dealing with something that is purely divine. In fact, it worth pointing out that this was the only light seen in the Holy Place. Jesus said, "I am the light of the world." He also said Christians are the light of the world. While Jesus is pictured in the lampstand, I believe the primary fulfilment of this type is the word of God.

You will remember that famous scripture from Psalms, "Your word is a lamp unto my feet and a light unto my path." Psalm 119:105.

There are no windows or light sources in the Holy Place, so if you wanted to see the table of the showbread or minister at the altar of incense, then it was the lampstand that gave you the ability to do so. Therefore it is the word of God that sheds light upon our walk with the Lord today. It is God's word that brings us revelation and clarity concerning the person and the work of Jesus Christ.

Flowers, Buds, And Blossoms.

Now here is a very cool confirmation that this lampstand speaks of the word of God. God instructed Moses to make a lampstand (The Menorah) that had seven branches. Three branches on each side of the centre branch, and on each of the branches, there were to be 3 cups (in the form of flowers), and each cup had buds and blossoms. The centre branch had 4 cups with each cup again having buds and blossoms. Do not be drifted off, but stay with me because this is where it gets interesting. The total number of decorations on each of the outer branches is, therefore, nine (9) cups (3 cups/flowers, 3buds, and 3 blossoms). The total number of decorations in the centre branch is twelve (12), (4 cups/flowers, 4 buds, and 4 blossoms). So, the overall total number of decorations (taking into account all seven branches) is $9+9+9+12+9+9+9=66$. Why 66? Because the lampstand is a type (picture) of the word of God and there are 66 books in God's word, the Bible, that gives light to all that would read and study its words. But also look at the split. If we take the first four branches, we get 39 ($9+9+9+12$). There are 39 books in the Old Testament. The remaining 3 branches give us 27 ($9+9+9$) which speaks of the 27 books in the New Testament. That is pretty amazing. Remember that the lampstand was made of pure gold, meaning the Bible is a divinely inspired book.

Keep That Light Shinning

The last thing I would like to draw your attention to concerning the lampstand in the Holy Place is a passage in Leviticus 24:1-4. "The Lord said to Moses, command the Israelites to bring you clear oil of pressed olives for the light so that the lamps may be kept burning continually. Outside the curtain of the Testimony in the Tent of meeting, Aaron is to tend the lamps before the Lord from evening till morning continually. This is to be a lasting ordinance for the generation to come. The lamps on the pure gold lampstand before the Lord must be tended continually." Leviticus 24:1-4.

The lampstand would give light, but oil was required to keep it burning. It was the task of Aaron to tend to the lamp to ensure that its wick was trimmed and that there was a fresh supply of oil. If there was no oil, there was no light. It is the same for the word of God. Oil is a picture of the Holy Spirit who has been given by our High Priest (Jesus Christ) to illuminate the word of God for us. The revelation and light that the word of God gives depends upon the oil.

Just as the outer court spoke of Salvation, so we have seen that each of the items in the Holy Place speaks to us concerning our fellowship and life in Christ. In one aspect, each of the items speaks of Christ. Jesus is the showbread that we feed upon, He is our High Priest who intercedes for us (the altar of incense), and He is the light that gives us life. The Holy Place also speaks to us of our need to feed upon Christ, to pray and intercede, and to receive the revelation of God's ways through the light of His word.

The Altar Of Incense- Exo.30:1-8

As you look around the Holy Place, the next item that takes your attention is the altar of incense which is made again from acacia wood with gold overlaid.

This altar was used by Aaron, the High Priest, for the burning of incense every day, morning and evening. Do you know what incense is in the bible? It is a picture (type) of prayer. So, let me ask you a question if you will be so kind. If Aaron had to offer incense morning and evening each day, in what way does this picture Jesus? Do not forget that Aaron was the High Priest, and He was a picture, type, shadow of Jesus, our High Priest today. As Aaron offered up the incense (a type of intercession) each day, so this picture the present-day work of Jesus on our behalf. "But He, because He continues forever, has an unchangeable Priesthood. Therefore...." Hebrews 7:24-25. So, the brazen altar that stood in the outer court speaks of the sacrifice of Jesus 2000 years ago to provide salvation for all who would believe. The golden altar in the Holy Place, however, speaks of the present work of the living resurrected Christ, who intercedes on behalf of His people. Just as we are fed on Christ (the table of showbread) so as priests before the Lord, we also offer up prayers, intercession, and praise. And just as the fire burnt continually on the Altar of incense, the New Testament tells us to pray continually. 1 Thess.5:17.

The Holy Of Holies

The outer court with the brazen altar and laver spoke of the means of salvation that is available in Christ. The Holy Place, on the other hand, spoke of fellowship and the means of growth in the Christian life. Now we shall investigate the final remaining area in the tabernacle, and that is the Holy of Holies. The outer court showed us that Jesus is the way, the Holy Place showed us that Jesus is the truth. But the Holy of Holies will give us a glimpse of Jesus as our life. It is the very presence and power of God that was present within the Holy of Holies, and it is that same presence that is essential to living the Christian life today.

"You shall make a veil of blue and twisted linen, it shall be with cherubim, the work of a skilful workman...." Exo.26:31-34

Now, put yourself in the position of the High Priest, while in the Holy Place. You look to view the Holy of Holies, and you see an amazing veil made from twisted linen, blue, purple and scarlet. This veil separates the Holy Place from the Holy of Holies. Knowing the use of these colours, you recognise that they represent the entrance into a heavenly (blue) royal (purple) and redemptive (scarlet) area, for beyond this veil is the presence of the King. It is only the High Priest who goes beyond this veil once a year during the day of atonement. Remember, this veil was torn in two the moment Jesus yielded up His Spirit on the cross of Calvary.

"And Jesus cried out again with a loud voice and yielded up His Spirit. And behold the veil of the temple was torn in two from the bottom, and the earth shook, and the rocks were split."

— Matthew 27:50-51.

A PLACE TO FIND MERCY - Beyond The Veil

"You shall put the Mercy Seat on top of the Ark, and in the Ark you shall put the testimony which I will give to you....."

— Exo 25:21-22

The Ark of the covenant represented the very presence of God, as the above verses mentioned, it is there that the Lord met with the High Priest. In fact, the whole tabernacle was constructed just to house the Ark of the covenant so that God could dwell among man. But how could a holy God dwell among sinful men. Well, the High Priest had to sprinkle the blood of the sacrifice upon the Mercy seat so that the sins of the nation could be atoned for. This had to occur every year. Now the amazing thing is that this earthly tabernacle was only a type (a picture) a copy of the very real heavenly tabernacle which Jesus entered following His death.

> *"But Christ came as High Priest of the good things to come, with the greater and more perfect tabernacle not made with hands, that is, not of this creation...."*
>
> **— Hebrews 9:11-12.**

> *"And according to the law, almost all things are purified with blood, and without shedding of blood there is no remission....."*
>
> **— Hebrews 9:22-24.**

Jesus entered the heavenly tabernacle by His own blood, and in typology to the earthly high priest (Aaron), Jesus sprinkled His blood upon the heavenly mercy seat to make eternal redemption and atonement. The impact of this act is given to us in the book of Romans and Hebrews amongst others.

Hebrews 9:3-4 tells us that there were objects placed within the ark. Each object speaks of a different aspect of Jesus Christ.

The Manna

That which has been the perfect food, containing all that the Israelites required to sustain them in their entire journey through the wilderness was in the ark. The manna was God's provision until they reached the promised land, and Jesus Christ is God's provision today. He is the one who sustains and strengthens us on our journey. As Jesus said, "Truly, truly, I say to you, it is not Moses who has given you the bread out of heaven. For the bread of God is that which comes down out of heaven, and gives life to the world.....I am the bread of life, he who comes to Me will not hunger, and he who believes in Me will never thirst." John 6:32-35.

Aaron Budding Rod

The second object placed in the Ark was Aaron's rod, and it was just an ordinary rod. Well ordinary apart from the fact that it budded flower and brought almonds. That a dead rod could produce fruit is a miracle. It speaks of the resurrection life; it speaks of the one who though died, came back to life after three days. And it is this resurrection life that God grants believers today. Death can no longer have a hold on them just as it could not contain their Saviour, for the one who has defeated death is the one who now dwells within the believer by His Spirit.

Tablets Of Stone

The next object within the ark was the stone tablets upon which God had written the 10 commandments with His own finger. These tablets within the ark of the covenant speak to us of the one and the only one who has ever kept the law of God and its entirety. They speak to us of the one who said, "Then I said, Behold, I have come - In the volume of the book it is written of Me - To do Your will, O God."-Hebrews 10:7.

The scripture declares that despite all the difficulties that the devil threw at Him, Jesus was yet without sin. "For we do not have a High Priest who cannot sympathise with our weaknesses, but One who has been tempted in all things as we are, yet without sin. Hebrews 4:15.

The tabernacle teaches us about sin, judgement, sacrifice, and salvation. But importantly, it teaches us about Jesus. He is God's gift to this world. Jesus fulfils all the pictures, shadows in the earthly tabernacle.

Beloved, when a person's focus is shifted from Christ Jesus with the belief that objects such as rods, horns, salt, candles, and similar things have power to make him or her free, then the person will be exhibiting his or her ignorance before the devil. The adversary roars like a lion seeking for the ignorant, the greedy and the desperate to devour. Be informed, and throw away the old Judaism way of worship and magic away, and take Christ Jesus, the author and finisher of our faith. May the God of our Lord Jesus Christ, the Father of glory grant you the Spirit of wisdom and revelation in the knowledge of Him. May this chapter help you greatly.

CHAPTER 6

WHY JESUS WAS MANIFESTED

In 1 John 3:8, the Son of God (Jesus) was manifested, that He might destroy the works of the devil. The day Adam ate the forbidden fruit, he and his offspring surely died as God had told him in the garden of Eden, but Adam lived for 930 years afterwards, so what kind of death was God talking about?

There are three kinds of death which the Bible talks about:

1. Spiritual Death

It is when the spirit of man is separated from God.

2. Physical Death

It is when the spirit of man is separated from his physical body.

3. Eternal Death

It is when the spirit of man is separated from God (his source) forever.

So, the kind of death that God told Adam was a spiritual death, that is the spirit of man separating from his source, God. This kind of death as a result, brought about physical death and all kinds of curses such as fear, lack, poverty, and such-like. As a fish will die when it is taken out of water (its source), and a plant will also die when it is uprooted from the soil (its source), so also man dies when he is cut off from his source (God). The day that Adam ate that forbidden fruit we instantly died spiritually, we were cut off from our source, and we became enemies to our God because we did not know Him, and not only that, we also lost all the power, the blessings and the power to increase that were entrusted into our care in the garden of Eden. By obeying the devil, Adam on a platter of silver relinquished the power and dominion to the devil, and man could not operate the way God intended him to. The day that you lost your child, job or that valuable pearls was not your saddest moment in life, but it was the day Adam ate that forbidden fruit. That disobedience (sin) affected the entire human race because we were right there in Adam. The scripture says as one man's disobedience made us all sinners, so also one man's (Christ) obedience has made us righteous.

Christianity means going back to the original. Original of what? In Genesis 1:26-28, the scripture says God created man in His own image and likeness. God blessed man and told him to have dominion over everything on earth and also have the power to multiply or increase. This was the original state of man from the beginning.

When a person puts his trust in Jesus and His finished work on the cross, he is translated from his old Adamic state of weaknesses, curses, and death into God's power, blessings, increase, and life abundance. As a man confesses with his mouth and believes in his heart that God raised Jesus from the dead, the scripture says that person is moved from the kingdom of darkness into God's marvellous light. That person is translated from eternal death into God's life eternal. Romans 10:9-10.

The Mystery Behind Christ First Coming

If anyone be in Christ, the scripture says he is a new creation, old things are passed away, behold, all things have become new. The moment we put our trust in Christ Jesus, the old things such as fear, curses, death give way to dominion, blessings, increase and power, but there is more to that.

> *"God has told us His secret reason for sending Christ, a plan He decided on in mercy long ago, and this was His purpose: that when the time is ripe, He will gather us all together from wherever we are in heaven or on earth to be with Him in Christ, forever."*
>
> — Ephesians 1:9-10. TLB

There is nothing greater than being a new creation with the power, blessings, and dominion being restored, but as I said earlier, there is something more to that. Apostle Paul in the above scripture is saying there is a secret (mystery) for God to send Jesus, and because it is a secret many people do not know. Inasmuch as we have the power back, this present world is coming to an end very soon. The time for this world to be destroyed is very near, as a matter of fact, we live in a borrowed time. In the days of Noah, Sodom and Gomorrah, some families were saved and some destroyed, in the same way, God is going to save a certain family, the called-out ones (the Church) before the destruction takes place. A campaign therefore, is going on and people are being saved each passing day. The question is, have you been saved? Have you registered for the new coming Jesus Government? When the trumpet sounds, would you be part of God's people who will be raptured? Many people I have come across attend church service because they want God to prosper them financially and give them other material things, which I also believe because He is Jehovah Jireh, the Lord, our provider. Others also attend church because they want healing for their bodies, praise God! He will because He is Jehovah Ropheka, the Lord our Healer. Jesus was manifested to destroy the works of the devil including sicknesses, diseases, lack, failure and disappointment and such-like. However, the primary reason (the main reason, the principal and the greatest reason) why Jesus was manifested was to save the spirit man (the inner man). And once the inner man is saved into God's Kingdom, the prosperity and the healing we are looking for would be taken care of. Jesus says, seek first God's Kingdom and He will add to you the things that you need. Again, Jesus told His disciples, not to rejoice because demons were subject to them, but they should rejoice because their names were written in heaven. Jesus was simply saying it is useless to display power and wealth here on earth and not having your spirit man saved. What will it profit a man if he gains everything here on earth and loses his soul?

The Sin Nature

The scriptures say, "For all have sinned, and come short of the glory of God." Romans 3:23. "The wages of sin is death." Romans 6:23. "Wherefore, just through one man sin entered the world, and death through sin, and thus death spread to all men because all sinned." Romans 5:12

The above scriptures point to the fact that we were sinners before we were born, and not because we were smokers, gossipers, thieves and such-like that made us sinners, but we inherited this sin from our great grandfather Adam when we were in our mother's womb.

Now this sinful nature, Adamic nature or old man cannot inherit the kingdom of God or enter heaven, and therefore, the need to get rid of it. "Jesus answered and said to him most assuredly, I say to you unless one is born again, he cannot see the kingdom of God."

How can this Sin nature be removed? And who can remove it? In short, how can one be born again? The scripture says in Romans 10:9-10, when a person believes in his heart and confess with his mouth that Jesus is Lord and that God raised Him from the dead on the third day from the grave, instantly and spiritually the blood of Jesus that was shared on the cross of Calvary removes that Adamic sin nature and makes the person a new creation (born again). It is only the blood of Jesus, and the emphasis is, the blood of Jesus, that can remove that Adamic sin nature. "Neither is there salvation in any other, for there is no other name under heaven given among men, by which we must be saved"- Acts 4:12.

What Really Happened On The Cross Of Calvary

"Your old evil desires were nailed to the cross with Him, that part of you that love to sin was crushed and fatally wounded, so that your sin-loving body is no longer under sin's control, no longer needs to be a slave to sin."-Romans 6:6.

"For He made Him who knew no sin to be sin for us, that we might become the righteousness of God in Him"

— 2 Corinthians 5:21

Justification

What really happened on the cross according to Romans 6:6, was that the old man (the sin nature), if not dealt with, leads man to eternal death, but thank God, Jesus on the cross of Calvary crushed this sin nature to death. Jesus on the cross destroyed this sin nature or the old man, and anyone who will believe in the finished work on the cross is saved. In the theological arena it is called justification, which means to be declared righteous (having right standing with God). Again on the cross, what happened was that God took our sins and poured them into Jesus, and in exchange, poured Christ's righteousness into us - 2Cor.5:21. Anyone who has faith in Christ's finished work on the cross is blood washed, sin nature crucified, the person is born again, and getting ready to enter into heaven.

But Pastor If The Sin Nature Was Crucified On The Cross Of Calvary Why Do We Sin After We Are Born-Again?

This is a great question that needs to be answered thoroughly. When Jesus on the cross said it is finished, yes, it was finished indeed. The scripture says a soldier pierced His side with a spear, and immediately blood and water came out. God needed the blood of Jesus to cleanse mankind (a Principle). The finished work on the cross crushed the sin nature (the old man) to death. However, when the old man was going, he left residual sins in our minds and bodies, and these residual sins continue to fight the new creation man.

"It seems to be a fact of life that when I want to do what is right, I inevitably do what is wrong. I love to do God's will so far as my new nature is concerned: but there is something else deep within me, in my lower nature, that is at war with my mind and wins the fight and make me a slave to the sin that is still

within me. In my mind, I want to be God's willing servant but instead, I find myself still enslaved to sin. So, you see how it is: my new life tells me to do right, but the old nature that is still inside me loves to sin, Oh, what a terrible predicament I'm in! Who will free me from my slavery to this deadly lower nature? Thank God! It has been done by Jesus Christ our Lord. He has set me free."

— Romans 7:21-25.

The above scripture teaches us of a born-again, blood washed, sin nature crushed Christian still struggling with sin. The question is where did this sin come from which is still deep within this Christian lower nature (body), which continues to war in the mind and wins the fight? His new creation life tells him to do what is right, but the old nature that is still inside tells this new born again Christian to sin. The reality of the matter is, the sin nature (the old man) was nailed to the cross with Jesus, the evil nature was crushed and fatally wounded as the scripture says in Rom.6:6. The Greek word for this sin is "Harmatia," and it was this sin nature that we inherited from Adam that Jesus crushed on the cross. When the Bible talks of: "the wages of 'sin' is death..., for all have 'sinned'..., wherefore, as by one man 'sin'...", God was referring to the sin nature "Harmatia." And it is this sin nature (Harmatia) that brought death and sends man to hell if not checked. Then we have another sin, which in the Greek is "Harmatano," which is the residual sins the old man left behind in our mind before he was crushed on the cross. It is these residual sins (harmatano) which are found in our lower nature (minds and bodies) that the scripture talks about. It is this residual sins (harmatano) that is still within the new creation Christians' mind and body which is at war and tries to win the fight, as stated in Romans 7:21-23.

Any person who puts his trust in Jesus Christ as his Lord and personal saviour is a born again Christian whose sin nature (Harmatia) has been crushed and fatally wounded. That person is a potential candidate waiting patiently to enter into heaven. This new creation Christian is righteous and operates under God's grace and not the law. Again, this new creation Christian is free from sin, condemnation, and death as stated in Romans 8:1. The new creation Christian now lives under a new law called the law of the Spirit of life in Christ Jesus. Nevertheless, the new creation Christian is still battling with residual sins," harmatano" such as fear, anger, jealousy, and such-like. Though these residual sins would not make the new creation Christian lose his salvation, it is an obligation or a command from God for the new creation to live according to the Spirit. For the new creation Christian to live a life with meaning and significance, the person must mortify the deeds of the flesh (harmatano) and be prepared to live according to the Spirit to avoid a defeated life instead of a victorious Christian life here on earth. Let me also state that the fight going on in your mind between your new man and your body is an indication that you are a Christian, do not give up the fight but just depend on the Holy Spirit to help you to overcome those residual sins. Very important brethren.

Sanctification

How does a new creation Christian put to death the deeds of the flesh and live according to the Spirit?

1. The first resource the Bible mentions in our effort to overcome the residual sins in our lives is the Holy Spirit. Pastor Andrew Wommack said, "two dogs fight, who wins? the one you feed." The way to deal

and overcome these residual sins which are at war with us is to feed the Spirit inside you with spiritual diets such as prayer and fasting, reading and studying of God's word, praising and worshipping God, attending church services and fellowship with Christians. By so doing, we give the Spirit the freedom to work within our thoughts and actions. If sins are what grieves the Spirit and hinders His work, then obedience to God's word will enable Him to operate on our behalf. The scripture says, for if by the Spirit we put to death the deeds of the flesh, we shall live. Walking in the Spirit daily, that is yielding to His leading, choosing to constantly follow the Holy Spirit promptings in our lives rather than following the flesh.

2. The second resource the scriptures mentioned in our effort to deal with these residual sins is the word of God. God has given us His word to equip us for every good work - 2 Timothy 3:16-17. Joshua was told that the key to success in overcoming his enemies was not to forget this resource but instead meditate on it day and night, and obey it. God's word is the weapon that the Spirit of God uses to fight. Ephesians 6:17

3. The third crucial resource in our battle against these residual sins is prayer. Again, it is a resource that Christians often give lip service to, but make poor use of it. We have prayer meetings, times of prayer, etc. but we do not use prayer in the same way as the early church. Acts 3:1, Acts 4:31, 6:4. In the garden of Gethsemane, Jesus told the disciples to watch and pray else they fall into temptation. Prayer is not a magic formula. It is simply acknowledging our own limitations

and God's inexhaustible power and turning to Him for that strength to do what He wants us to do.

4. A fourth resource in our war to conquer the residual sins is the church, the fellowship with other believers. The missionaries in Acts did not go out one at a time but in groups of two or more. The Bible commands us not to forsake the assembling of the saints, using the time to encourage one another in love and good works - Hebrews 10:24. In the wisdom literature of the Old Testament, we are told that as iron sharpens iron, so one man sharpens another - Proverbs 27:17.

Sometimes victory over sin comes quickly, other times slowly. God has promised that as we make use of His resources, He will progressively bring about change in our lives. We can persevere in our efforts to overcome sin because we know that He is faithful to His promises.

The process of eliminating these residual sins (harmatano) in our lives in the theological arena is called Sanctification.

The Danger Of Residual Sins (Harmatano)

Where we are now in life is as a result of decisions and the choices we made yesterday. There was this woman when angry speaks anyhow, so the husband left home due to the wife's character, and for more than ten years did not show up. She then married again to a younger man and even went to the extent of sponsoring this man's education and other financial obligations, just to win him to herself, but it did not work either due to her attitude. This desperate woman still in search of a husband decided to take her ordeal into prayer, so she moved from one prayer camp to another but to no avail. "Woman, the truth of the matter is, though you are a Christian, you are living according to the flesh, and the spirit of anger has taken a greater part of your life and has destroyed your marriage twice. Know that anger is the cause and until you ask the Holy Spirit to help you deal with it forget about marriage," I told her. She took the counselling seriously and with prayer, the word of God and her commitment to the church, God blessed her with a husband after two years, and the good news is that they have been living happily as husband and wife for the past seven years. Residual sins, if not checked could bring a believer's life or a whole nation to a perpetual disgrace and defeat, which I call delivered but wondered. Selah.

There are more Christians in Africa than any other continent according to a report released by "The Christian Post" on July 11, 2018. And it reads, "More Christians now live in Africa than any other continent in the world. Recent data reveals that for the first time, Africa is now home to the greatest number of Christians in the world. Latin America held that title previously. An infographic provided by the Centre for the Study of Global Christianity at Gordon-Conwell Theological Seminary shows that more than 631 million Christians currently reside in Africa, and they make up 45 percent of the population. Latin America is estimated to have 601 million Christians." John Paul Sunico, Christian Post Coordinator.

As of 2016, North America has the highest GDP per capita, and Africa has the lowest among the world's continent according to a report by the IMF

North America:

"North America continent has a multifaceted economic system and the highest GDP per capita according to the International Monetary Fund 2016 report. The continent had a commutative GDP of about $120 trillion against a population of 360 million people. The continent had a GDP per capita (nominal) of US$37,477 in 2016. The US is the largest economy in North America accounting for over 85% of the continent's gross domestic product."

"AFRICA: The continent with the lowest GDP per capita. Africa is the poorest continent according to GDP per capita. Most of the top ten poorest countries are in Africa with the majority having per capita GDP of less than $1500. Africa has an average GDP per capita of $1809, the lowest in the seven continents."

A continent dominated by Christians with poverty rate so high is unacceptable, and a disgrace to our Christianity and this needs an urgent redress.

The mathematician El Khamarov said, " poverty is like punishment for a crime you did not commit." He stated that some of the factors that bring about poverty and hardships to man are: dictatorial and corrupt government, weak rule of law, war and social unrest. A beautiful continent endowed with rich natural resources, but dictatorship, corruption, lies, greediness have changed the destiny of mother Africa. A Christian continent but walk after the flesh, we kick against God's word by failing to take God at His word (hypocrisy), but we should not forget that the scriptures cannot be broken. It is about time to say we are sick and tired of hardships and repent, mortify the deeds of the flesh and walk after the Spirit. Brethren, we should not go to heaven in poverty, lack, sicknesses, diseases, and failure, but wage war against these residual sins which are in our lower nature (body), if we want to live a life with meaning and significance as an individual or a nation.

The Danger Of Living Contrary To God's Word

Bob Marley, the reggae music legend said, "So much trouble in the world." So much troubles in the world, nations, homes, offices, and streets. Troubles from terrorism, climate change, earthquakes, hurricanes etc. Troubles from lack, sicknesses, and diseases, so much troubles in the world. The peace of God that surpasses human understanding seems to elude man each passing day, and it is because we have not known the truth or rejecting the truth. And when a truth is not known or rejected, deception, error, and suffering are inevitable.

Jesus in Matthew 22:29, told those Jews, "You are deceived because you don't know the scriptures or the power of God." It is dangerous and disturbing to be a Christian and not knowing the scriptures or the power of God. The fact of the matter is that Satan our adversary operates in a vacuum (dark or empty vessels), and his deception catches innocent Christians who have not got the scriptures rooted in them or ignorant about the word of God. Satan's strategy is to keep the believer away from the 'Truth' so that he can deceive man with his signs and deceiving wonders. I want to repeat by saying that people troop to go and watch magic and deceiving wonders, and call it church service. Wealth is displayed through magic in such meetings to sway the desperate and ignorant to follow Satan, and at that moment the deceived neglect and forget about praying or depending on God for his or her supply, and when Satan captures the minds of the people through deceiving signs and wonders, his mission is accomplished.

Principles About Prayer

When we study the scriptures carefully, we will realise that Jesus earthly ministry was about prayer, prayer, and prayer, always in touch with the Father in heaven. He will pray all night to solve peoples' problems all day. Do we have problems at hand? If the answer is yes, then let us emulate what the Son of man did.

What Is Prayer Then?

Let us see how some brethren defined it.

"Prayer is about seeking God's face and having communion with Him."

"Prayer is depending on God."- by Pastor Joseph Prince.

"Prayer is when the believer begins to exercise his legal authority to invoke heaven's influence on earth."- by Dr. Myles Munroe.

"Prayer is communion with God. It is the closest, most intimate relationship you can have with the creator. Prayer is not playing magic games, spinning prayer wheels, reading off a list, or asking of things to be done. It's a communion, Deep calls deep; the scripture says - Psalm 42:7. In prayer, the depths of your spirit are in communion with the depths of the Spirit of God. Out of this can come instructions, guidance, or a burden to pray for certain things."

The Significance Of Prayer

Man is a spirit, he has a soul and lives in a body. During prayer, it is the spirit man who communicates with God who is a Spirit. As a matter of fact, the flesh is always at war with the spirit when it comes to spiritual things like fasting and prayer, however for a Christian to have a victorious life here on earth he or she needs to depend on God (his source) who is a Spirit through prayer. When we stop praying, we indirectly announce our independence from God, we are simply saying we can do it by ourselves. Prayer, therefore, is depending on God, as pastor Joseph Prince puts it.

In John gospel chapter 15:5, Jesus says He is the vine, and we are the branches, He goes on to advise us to abide in Him, and He in us, for without Him we can do nothing. That is until we depend on Him, we should forget about success or victory. Someone said, life without Christ is full of crisis.

Double Kingdom Rule

> *" In the third year of king Cyrus of Persia, a message was revealed to me Daniel, whose name was called Belteshazzar. The message was true, but the appointed time was long and he understood the message, and had understanding of the vision."*
>
> — **Daniel 10:1**

> *"But the Prince of the kingdom of Persia withstood me twenty-one days and behold, Michael, one of the chief princes, came to help me, for I had been left alone there with the kings of Persia."*
>
> — **Daniel 10:13.**

In Daniel chapter 10:1, we see Cyrus king of Persia. This king Cyrus was a physical king who was ruling the then world in Persia on earth. In Daniel chapter 10:13, we see the prince of the kingdom of Persia. This prince of the kingdom of Persia was a spiritual being, who ruled the kingdom of Persia from the second heavens. The prince of the kingdom of Persia was a spirit being who controlled Cyrus king of Persia who was a mortal physical king on earth. That is to say, the prince of the kingdom of Persia, a spirit being in the second heavens, was more powerful than Cyrus the king of Persia on earth. Again, Cyrus the king of Persia, took counsel and instructions from the prince of the kingdom of Persia.

So also Christians, we are commanded to live and act according to the advises and instructions (principles) of our God, who is in the third heavens. The reason is, things in heaven are spiritual and are powerful compared to things here on earth. The earth is heaven's annex, and therefore failure to comply with their instructions will see one's life crumbled. Heaven principle says we should call on our God in heaven, and He will answer us and show us great and mighty things, which we do not know. Heaven says, is anyone among you suffering, that person should keep on praying about it.

> *"Assuredly I say to you, whatever you bind on earth will be bound in heaven and whatever you loose on earth will be loosed in heaven."*
>
> **— Matthew 18:18**

My understanding of this scripture is that heaven is waiting on our prayer to act on our behalf. When prayer is released from here on earth heaven acts on it accordingly. This confirms Dr. Myles Munroe's prayer definition which says, " when the believer begins to exercise his legal authority to invoke heaven's influence on earth." Beloved do not stop praying, for it is the key to our victory, and until we petition God and bring Him into the equation we are doomed. On the other hand, if we can commune with God on a regular basis, and take Him at His word, victory will be ours, for we are just God's containers, and God is our content.

Kinds Of Prayers And Their Significances

"And pray in the spirit on all occasions with all kinds of prayers and request. With this in mind, be alert and always keep on praying for all the Lord's people."

— **Ephesians 6:18 NIV**

The Truth About Praises And Worship

1.Prayer of Praise and Worship - Psalm 761-3, Ps 100:1-4, Isa 6:1-3

What does the truth say about praises and worship and its significance to the believer? Brethren, the prayer of praises and worship is so important to the believer so much that the adversary wants to keep us away from it.

The Greek word for worship is "proskuneo" which literally means to bow down to kiss someone, to throw a kiss as a token of respect or homage, to adore and show respect.

In the ancient oriental (especially Persia), the mode of salutation between persons of equal rank was to kiss each other on the lips. When the difference of rank was slight, they kissed each other on the cheek. When one was much inferior, he fell upon his knees, touch his forehead to the ground or prostrated himself, and as he is bowing down, he will be throwing kisses towards the superior. This type of greetings is also practiced in Nigeria when a child is greeting the elderly. Worship which in Greek is proskuneo came to mean prostration, throwing oneself on the ground to show awe or respect before a deity. In the Septuagint Greek Old Testament, such worship was reserved for Jehovah God. In fact, it was considered sacrilege for a Jew to express worship towards any other pagan god or person. One recalls that Daniel's friends refused to bow to their ruler's idol - Daniel 3:1-12, and Mordecai also refused to bow to Haman the Agagite, Esther 3:2-5. As Christians, it is our duty-bound to praise and worship our God who is our creator, and the creator of the whole universe. In Him we live, move and have our being. He is the I AM that I AM, and therefore He needs to be worshipped. Worship tells God who He is, whilst praising Him is to call attention to His glory (the totality of God's goodness).

Significance In Praises And Worship To The Believer

"In Judah God is known, His name is great in Israel. In Salem also is His tabernacle. And His dwelling place in Zion. There He broke the arrows of the bow. The shield and sword of battle. Selah."

— Psalm 76:1-3.

The above scripture says God is known in Judah, and in Genesis chapter 29:35 teaches that Judah means praise. Therefore, God is known in praises. I keep telling brethren that Mr. Donald Trump is known in the United States, whilst Lionel Messi of Barcelona FC fame is known in Argentina or Barcelona FC. Now if someone wants to see these men, he has to go to the United States and Argentina or Spain respectively. So also, our God the scripture says is known in praises and could be seen at no other place than in praises and worship. In praises and worship, God is known, and He manifests His glory, and that His manifestation breaks all the arrows and bows (the weapons of the devil), such as sickness, lack, ignorance, etc. In the book of Acts chapter 16:25, when Paul and Silas were put in prison with their feet fastened in the stocks, the scripture says they prayed and sang hymns to God. The scripture went on to say that suddenly there was a great earthquake so that the foundation of the prison building shook, and immediately all the doors to the prison were opened and everyone's chains were loosed, due to the praises and worship that they offered unto God. When the praises go up, His glory will surely come down. When Christians sing praises and worship to God, we are not just entertaining ourselves in church but sending a message to invoke heaven's influence on earth concerning a matter.

In Isaiah 6:1-3, Isaiah said in the year that king Uzziah died, I saw the Lord sitting on a throne, high and lifted up, and His train (robe) filled the temple. Above it stood Seraphim, each one had six wings, with two he covered his face, with two he covered his feet, and with two he flew. And one cried to another and said Holy, Holy, Holy is the Lord of Host. The whole earth is full of His glory! Isaiah who was on earth saw what was going on in heaven. As the Seraphim began to worship the one who sits upon the throne, the scripture says God's glory filled the whole earth, my goodness! What is God's glory? It is the totality of God's goodness. Beloved, where the glory of God is, there is no sorrow, pain, anxiety, death and such-like. The spirit of bondage will always give way to liberty whenever God's glory surfaces, so also death will give way to life at the presence of God's glory, and such-like. It is, therefore, an established truth that it is better to die than to live without the glory of God. That was why the High Priest Eli chose to die than to live without the glory of

God, when the Ark of God, which in those days symbolised the glory of God, was captured by the Philistines - 1Samuel 4:17-18.

Beloved, praises and worship ought to go up to release God's glory, this kind of prayer is so important and crucial to Christians, because God's glory is needed to deal with the kingdom of darkness and spiritual wickedness in high places who are terrorising our lives.

Praises and worship is also a spiritual key the believer uses to open God's gate and gets to His court before a request is put before God. - Psalm 100:4.

Once Satan keeps people ignorant about this biblical principle of praises and worship, he continues to keep God's people in bondage. Take your praises and worship seriously, and do not let anyone fool or school you outside the Bible.

At the age of 8, I remember my grandmother told me, "Daniel, anytime you go to church after praises and worship, if it's possible, you better return home." "Why grandma?," I asked, "There are angels from heaven who come to take records "mark register" and go back to heaven immediately after praises and worship, all those who enter the temple after praises and worship are latecomers, and they are punished the way pupils are punished when they are late to school." What my grandma was trying to teach me was that all latecomers go back home with their problems, because it is during praises and worship that barriers and Jericho walls are broken and torn down by God's glory. That was the idea behind the answer my grandmother gave to me, and it has been with me, with Psalm 76:1-3 giving me a deeper understanding. During the time of praises and worship, may God break all the bows, arrows, and the spears the enemy has thrown against you, including lack, sickness and diseases, barrenness, failure, and such-like.

Prayer Of Supplication Or Request - Philippians 4:4-7

"Be anxious for nothing, but in everything by prayer and supplication with thanksgiving, let your request be made known to God."

The Greek word "request" here is "aiteo" meaning to ask something or make urgent petition to the point of demanding. According to Matthew 7:7, a Christian has the legal authority to put his request before God.

Prayer Of Intercession - James 5:16

Intercessory prayer is to pray for someone. In 1Peter 2:5, the scripture says we are a holy priesthood, and in 1 Peter 2:9, we are a royal priesthood. In Revelation 1:6 and 5:10, we have been made kings and priests and, therefore, the need to intercede for one another.

Significance

Christians seldom pray for one another due to lack of understanding. In the book of Job 42:10, the scripture makes a revelation on intercessory prayer. "And the Lord restored Job's losses when he prayed for his friends. Indeed, the Lord gave Job twice as much as he had before." May God restore you as you pray for one another, as you pray for those in government, and as you pray for the expansion of God's Kingdom here on earth.

Praying In The Spirit - 1corinthians 14:4, Romans 8:26

"Likewise the Spirit also helps in our weakness. For we do not know what we should pray for as we ought, but the Spirit Himself makes intercession for us with groanings which cannot be uttered."

We also pray in the spirit (in tongues) to build ourselves spiritually.-1Cor.14:4

Prayer Of Dedication-1 Samuel 1:11

Prayer of dedication is committing or giving back to God what He has given you. Let us look at Hannah's prayer at 1 Samuel 1:11. "Then she made a vow and said "O Lord of hosts, if You will indeed look on the affliction of Your maidservant and remember me, and not forget Your maidservant, But will give Your maidservant a male child, then I will give him to the Lord all the days of his life, and no razor shall come upon his heard."

In verse 25, " Then they slaughtered a bull, and brought the child to Eli."

Significance

After Hannah had brought Samuel to the high priest Eli, God blessed her again with three sons and two daughters. In Acts chapter 9:4, Jesus, on the road of Damascus asked: "Saul, Saul, why are you persecuting Me." Jesus did not say why are you persecuting my people or my church, but rather "Me."

Saul, who later became Apostle Paul, went blind after his encounter with Jesus. When we dedicate everything about us to the Lord, that thing or person becomes His, and therefore any spirit, power, or person who touches you unlawfully must face the consequence because the person has touched Jesus Himself. In Zechariah 2:8, the scripture says anyone who touches

God's property touches the apple of His eye. When we dedicate something to God, we are simply saying God bring increase and protection.

Prayer Of Faith-James 5:15

Pastor Joel Osteen said, "faith is the currency Christians use to purchase things from heaven." In the book of James chapter 1:6, the writer admonishes Christians to ask God in faith not doubting anything, for he who doubts is like a wave of the sea driven and tossed by the wind. For let no man suppose that he will receive anything from the Lord. Praying in doubt is like sowing peanuts in the field with a ground squirrel or chipmunk standing by. There won't be any harvest, not even germination, because the standby squirrel will eat every seed sown after the sower had gone. Christians should mortify that spirit of doubt and unbelief, for they neutralise prayers. When we pray with those spirits standing by, we are indirectly saying God is incapable of doing what He has promised, making Him a liar. Do not be afraid only believe and all will be well, Jesus told Jairus. My understanding here is that, if He created it then He can fix it, just make sure that what you are looking for does not contradicts with the Bible.

The Truth About The Word Of God

It is one thing to be born again, hallelujah! And another thing to renew the mind and live after the Spirit (taking God at His word). As we pray believing that God moves on our behalf, we should not forget to pray with the word of God, in the sense that the Holy Spirit who gives us victory has a sword that He fights with, and it's called the word of God. We should hold the word of God in high esteem always and pray, and the reason is, in the realm of the spirit, the word of God is like a gun that needs bullets (prayer) for battle. In the natural, a bullet without a gun cannot win a battle and vice versa. The same way prayer without the word of God is a non-starter; that was why Jesus earthly ministry was prayer, prayer, and prayer. He is the word but needed the power to do battle on earth.

If we want our prayers to bring us wonderful results, then we have to pray and live in the word of God at the same time. God answers prayer according to His word and promises and not our tears, for He watches over His word to perform the scripture says. In Exodus 2:24 "So God heard their groaning, and God remembered His covenant with Abraham, Isaac and with Jacob, verse 25 "And God looked upon the children of Israel, and God acknowledge them." The word of God and prayer move together; when we pray with the word, we remind God of His promises to us.

"The effective, fervent prayer of a righteous man avails much" James 5:16b. The Living Bible Version says," The earnest prayer of a righteous man has great power and wonderful results."

Now the question is, who is a righteous man? A righteous man is simply a person who has a right standing with God. A righteous man has a personal relationship with God, a person who seeks to obey God and yield to the directions of the Holy Spirit, a person who wants what is right and wants to see God's Truth and God's will established on this earth. The scripture says such a person's prayer carries great power to bring wonderful results. Therefore, we can say that there are some prayers which are not great and do not bring wonderful results. In the bible were some guys who gathered themselves to pray concerning a problem, but the more they prayed, the more the problem compounded.

".....But the Lord sent out a great wind on the sea, and there was a mighty tempest on the sea, so that the ship was about to be broken up. Then the mariners were afraid; and every man cried out to his god, and threw the cargo that was in the ship into the sea, to lighten the load. But Jonah had gone down into the lowest part of the ship, had lain down, and was fast asleep." Jonah 1:4-5.

"Nevertheless, the men rowed hard to return to land, but they could not, for the sea continued to grow more tempestuous against them. Therefore, they cried out to the Lord and said "we pray, O Lord, please do not let us perish for this man's life, and do not charge us with innocent blood; for You, O Lord, have done as it pleased you. So, they picked up Jonah and threw him into the sea, and the sea ceased from its raging." Jonah 1:13-15.

The prophet Jonah has rejected God's word, refusing to go to Nineveh and preach the word of repentance for the people to repent from their sins. Jonah then decided to run away from God's assignment, so he went to Joppa and boarded a ship that was heading towards Tarshish, but on the journey arose a great wind. The captain and the mariners did two things that did not work.

1. They prayed to their god.
2. They tried to apply their knowledge and experience in sailing by throwing the cargo into the sea to lighten the load, but it did not work either.

In Jonah 1:13, the mariners tried to save the ship and Jonah by rowing hard to return to land, but they could not. The scripture says the sea continued to grow more tempestuous against them. Their prayers could not solve the problem, their knowledge and experience in sailing could not help them either, and it was all because a Jew, a prophet of God, has violated God's word.

Jonah 1:15 says the sea ceased from its raging the moment they threw Jonah into the water. My suggestion is, Jonah should have told the captain to send him back to Joppa, and he would have complied, because Jonah had two options, either to go back to Joppa or thrown into the deep sea.

Brethren it is not worth it and does not help in any way when we embark on prayer and fasting and at the same time, violate God's word. God has magnified His word above all His name, the scripture says. When God speaks, it becomes a law or a principle which God Himself respects and cannot violate them; that is why the scripture says He watches over His word to perform. Meaning God does not perform outside His word.

> *"Now there was a man in their synagogue with unclean spirit. And he cried out, saying "let us alone! What have we to do with you, Jesus of Nazareth? Did you come to destroy us? I know who you are the Holy One of God!"*
>
> — **Mark 1:23-24.**

Satan and his demons believe, respect and tremble at God's word; they also know the power that the word carries, except that they do not practice what the word says. When a Christian walk in the word and pray, it's like putting a bullet in a gun, he holds a dangerous weapon and the enemy better hide else he follows the ancestors. Satan knowing this, first disarms the Christian of his gun (the word) before he can destroy. In the book of Luke 10:30, the scripture says the thieves stripped the man on the Jericho road garment before wounding him, leaving him half dead. Satan will first break your relationship with God, your covering before he can wound you, and that garment the devil removed symbolises the saints' righteousness (our right standing with God) - Rev.19:8. Again in Galatians 3:27, the scripture says, "as many as were baptised into Christ, have put on Christ." Every Christian has put on Christ, Christ is our battle cloth, and until the battle cloth (Christ) is removed, the enemy has no way. That is why in church we have bible classes and teachings, discipleship classes, new convert classes, etc. to equip (to know and stick to Christ the more) the believer. Any church which is not a word-based church has no reason to exist, and the time is now to go back to the Bible. The Bible is the gun, prayer is the bullet. The weapon that the Holy Spirit uses to fight is called THE WORD OF GOD - Ephesians 6:17

CHAPTER 7

JESUS HEALING WINGS

Prophetess Hadassah Anane Dankyi who has gone to be with the Lord once narrated to me her challenges in ministry, and it went like this: "Apostle Daniel, you know what, this ministry started more than twenty years ago, and we were much more than the number you see now. We started as a prophetic, deliverance and prayer ministry and most often did not open to read the Bible, and therefore it was not a bible teaching ministry. God one day told me to get focused and make the bible a priority else I deviate from the calling, so my husband who was then in the circular field, joined me fully in the ministry. He is a scholar, so the teaching and the preaching of the word went on very well, but when the congregation saw that the church was now focusing more on the word, surprisingly, more than half of the members stopped coming to church. Before our own eyes, we saw the people leaving just like that, but then we have to obey and please God and not men. By God's grace, the number we have now are well vested in the word of God, and we are proud of that. As I speak to you now, most of the members are on the preaching roster and are giving five to seven minutes to share with the church a word of exhortation every Sunday church service. God has been good to us all the time." She concluded.

The devil has been fighting against the truth from the garden of Eden, he tried to kill the truth (Jesus), in the wilderness, was against the truth after His resurrection, tried to use the soldiers to go and peddle lies that Jesus has not risen but the disciples by night came to steal His body. He is still in that business of telling lies and denying many from knowing the truth in this generation too. He is attacking the truth so much because he knows when men get to know the truth (Jesus) he will be exposed. Beloved, have you observed the present situation in our churches, that bible and discipleship classes these days have been attended by a few dedicated individuals, and whilst these teachings are going on, some even doze off? The present generation is looking for something quick, magic and not the process way of doing things. The enemy is sowing discords into many to thinking that God's principles do not work like before, a great deception and a fallacy. If the truth does not work then what else will work again?

Global climate change, terrorism, economic crisis, unemployment, and such-like could be solved by sticking to the truth (Jesus) - John 15:5. I have a strong conviction of what I am saying, that if it is the word of God that created the universe, then it will take the same word to fix it that which has gone wrong. It is about time to go back and seek solutions from the Lord (the owner) of this world. Reject God's word, and you have rejected the power and solution to crisis.

Let me explain this.

Healing In The Wings (The Word)

"And suddenly, a woman who had a flow of blood for twelve years came from behind and touched the hem of His garment. For she said to herself "if only I may touch His garment, I shall be made well. But Jesus turned around, and when He saw her, He said, be of good cheer, daughter; your faith has made you well. "And the woman was made well from that hour. "

— Matthew 9:20-22.

This miracle healing in the scripture tells us the story of a certain woman who had gone through agony with an issue of blood for twelve years without relief. The scripture says that she had spent all her money on cures, but none succeeded; instead her problem grew worse, but she had heard about Jesus the Messiah who could heal, so she anxiously sought Him out. According to the Levitical law in Leviticus 15:19-33, it was forbidden for her to do that, but she decided to defile the law and protocol. She then meandered her way through the multitudes, stooped and touched the hem of Jesus garment, and the scripture says immediately she was healed. The question here is, why did the woman touch no other place except the hem of Jesus garment? The woman could have touched the back, shoulder or the edge of Jesus' sleeves but she reached out and touched the hem of the garment.

The scriptures in Matthew 14:35-36 and Mark 6:56 state that wherever Jesus went the sick were healed by touching the hem of Jesus garment.

"And when the men of that place recognised Him, they sent out into all the surrounding region, brought to Him all who were sick, and begged Him that they might only touch the hem of His garment. And as many as touched it were made perfectly well." Matthew 14:35-36.

What was so significant about the hem of Jesus garment that could produce healing to the sick? Let me use scriptures to explain this.

"And the Lord spoke to Moses saying, speak to the children of Israel, tell them to make tassels at the corners of their garments throughout their generations and to put a blue thread in the tassels of the corners. And you shall have the tassels, that you may look upon it and remember all my commandments of the Lord and do them and that you may not follow the harlotry to which your own hearts and your own eyes are inclined, and that you may remember and do all my commandments, and be Holy for your God." Numbers 15:37-40.

"You Shall Make Tassels On The Four Corners Of Clothing Which You Will Cover Yourself."

— Deuteronomy 22:12.

God told Moses to tell the children of Israel to make tassels or fringes at the four corners, wings or hem of their garments and the tassels or fringes will remind them of God's commandments.

"Kanaf" in Hebrew is translated as; Wings, Corners, or Hem.

"Tzitzit" in Hebrew is translated as tassels or fringes with "Kraspedon" as it's Greek word and "Tekhelet," another Hebrew word is the blue thread in the tassels. Blue colour indicates something heavenly and divine. Please do not forget these.

In the ancient times, a Jewish man's clothing was essentially a long rectangular cloth that draped down over the body. It had four corners at the bottom, and this is where the Israelites were to attach these tassels or fringes. They were to put a blue thread symbolising something heavenly and divine in the tassels, and this was to remind them of the Lord's commandments, God's law (God's word) given to them. Over time, clothing styles changed, and robes became more rounded at the bottom, and no longer have four corners, so the Jews developed something called the "tallith" which means in Hebrew small tent. This is a Jewish prayer shawl, a rectangular woollen mantel with the tassels or fringes at the four corners, wings, or hem.

When Samuel rebuked Saul for failing to destroy all the Amalekites, Samuel turned to go, and Saul reached out to stop him. In doing so, he ripped the tassels from Samuel's garment. Samuel used this as a picture of what God was going to do with the kingdom of Israel. The kingdom was to be ripped out of Saul's grip. 1 Sam.15:27-28

When David cut off the bottom of Saul's garment, he cut off the tzitzit or the tassels. Saul's garment was seen as a symbol of his authority to reign as king.

When Elijah was taken up to heaven, Elisha was given Elijah's mantel. This was probably his 'tallith.''

Significance Of The Tassels/Fringes (The Word).

The tassels or fringes (tzitzit) are formed from seven white and one blue twisted string. Each tassel consists of eight threads and five knots, a total of thirteen elements. Six hundred(600) is the numerical value of the tzitzit with eight threads and five knots making a total of six hundred and thirteen(613) which points to the 613 commandments of the Torah that God gave to the children of Israel,"365 thou shall not "and "248 thou shall," that you may look upon it and remember all the commandments of the Lord. The colour white symbolises the purity of God and blue points to something heavenly and divine.

The tassels at the corners of a man's garment were there to be a constant reminder of his relationship to God and to God's law (the word). Since they were to be at the four corners of the garment, no matter which way he turned, he would be reminded of the law and of his responsibilities to the law.

"But to you who fear My name The Sun of Righteousness shall arise With healing in His wings; And you shall go out And grow fat like stall-fed calves."

— **Malachi 4:2.**

The above scripture indicates that there shall come a time that the Sun of Righteousness (Jesus) will arise, and there will be healing in His wings- corners, hem, or kanaf (Hebrew) in His garment.

When the woman with the issue of blood came from behind Jesus and touched the hem of His garment, she was embracing the promise of Malachi 4:2. She was looking for healing in His wings (corners or hem). The woman touched the 613 commandments in the Torah, simply she touched the word of God. I believe that there was a revelation given to this woman by the Holy Spirit to apply Mal.4:2, and therefore that touch was not an ordinary touch, but a spiritual touch, it was a calculated touch of healing, it was a touch of faith and obedience.

Revelation Touch

It was a revelation touch in the sense that Malachi 4:2 has been there in the books for reading and studying long before the Sun of Righteousness, but it did not occur to any of them to apply it, not even the Pharisees or the High Priest understood it, until it was revealed to this poor, miserable and rejected woman. It was a revelational touch because Peter and his colleagues did not even understand the kind of touch Jesus was talking about, except the Holy Spirit, Jesus and the woman.

" ..Master, the multitudes throng and press You, and You say, 'Who touched Me?' But Jesus said, "Somebody touched Me, for I perceived power going out of Me." Now when the woman saw that she was not hidden, she came trembling, and falling down before Him, she declared to Him in the presence of all the people the reason she had touched Him and how she was healed immediately." Luke 8:45-47.

When the woman touched the hem, corners, or the wings of His garment it was the same as touching Him or the word of God because Jesus is the word of God, and the word of God is Jesus. The woman looked to Jesus by faith, and when her faith touched His grace she was healed. She was claiming the promises of the word of God and resting in the grace of God. She came to the right person in the right manner and she got what she wanted.

Touch Of Faith

It was a touch of faith that produced healing, " For she said to herself, if only I may touch His garment, I shall be made well."

After the woman had received the revelation of Mal.4:2, she believed and acted, that brought about her healing. Rahab the prostitute, after hearing the wondrous things that God had done for Israel, acknowledged Him, and because of her reverence and acknowledgment to God, she and her family were saved.

Beloved, I believe it is about time to say enough is enough, and that we are sick and tired of this life of uncertainty and go for Christ, and we will receive the needed solution for our lives. Jesus the creator and the Saviour of the world, let us call upon Him, and He will answer us and even show us great and mighty things we do not know. My heart desire and prayer to God is that the hearts of men will be flooded with light so that they can see and understand who Christ really is. Beloved He is the Lord (owner) of the whole universe because He created all things and therefore has solution to every problem. And until the world comes to that knowledge and understanding we will be moving in circles.

A Young Woman's Agony

One day a young woman came and narrated to me her agony with regards to her marriage with her pastor. That the pastor promised to marry her but somewhere along the line had slept with her, and since then, this pastor hates her to the extent that he does not want to see her presence. I opened the scriptures and counselled her from Ammon and Tamar's story which went very well with her.

"Then Ammon hated her exceedingly, so that the hated with which he hated her was greater than the love with which he had loved her. And Ammon said to her, Arise, be gone!"

— 2 Samuel 13:15.

I told her, "young woman, you have sinned against God, and since sin does not add but subtracts, it has solicited for hatred from the man who promised to marry you. Nevertheless, our God and Father is a God of another opportunity, for the scripture says," "If we say we have no sin, we deceive ourselves, and the truth is not in us. If we confess our sins. He is faithful and just to forgive us our sins and to cleanse us from all unrighteousness."1 John 1:8-9.

"But God who is rich in mercy because of His love with which He loved us."

— Ephesians 4:2.

With these scriptures, I counselled and prayed for her and told her to keep herself pure and by God's grace and mercy the man will show up again. Within three weeks, this young woman called me on the phone to inform me that the man has come back and had pleaded for forgiveness, and has also asked her to join him for a shopping. "Keep yourself pure and a little distance from him till he marries you will help you," I told her. Two months later, this woman came to me dejected, and the problem was that the man had forced her again to bed leaving bruises on her body, but again I counselled and prayed for her. A year later, I met this woman and she was pregnant. "Are you now married" I asked expecting a positive answer from her, but she replied, "Apostle no, I am far from getting married." The man has impregnated her (fornication), and after that thrown her out of the house and now going out with another woman.

Beloved, one cannot reject God's word and come out successful in this battle of life. This woman was indeed far from getting married, and it was because she took God's word for granted. Jesus in John 6:63 says, "....the words that I speak to you are spirit, and life."

When we do what God entreats us not to do, we tie His hands, and we prevent Him from reaching us thereby causing our own defeat in life. For there is no way the enemy can defeat us as Christians except by policies of consensus and compromise. Dr. Myles Munroe said, "whenever God speaks, we need to listen carefully because we are about to receive His revealed intentions." And any act of disobedience to God's word lengthens the distance between us and our dream, and therefore, if we want to live a life with meaning and significance then we need to give reverence and acknowledgment to His principles (word).

Living Testimony

Let me conclude this chapter with this testimony. A brother of Grace Outreach Church for three weeks was absent in church, so one Sunday after church service I went to the house just to verify what was keeping him from coming. His reason was that, he had been a devoted Christian paying his tithe and offering believing God, yet his heart desire has not been met, so he decided to stay back home and see what the future has for him. I counselled and prayed for him, so we saw him in church the following Sunday. Three months later, he came and told me he has a living testimony to tell. "What is it," I asked. He has bought a brand-new Benz 250 which I prophesied to him some time ago.

God's word does not fail; if we can mix it with faith, it will always profit us. There are solutions in the wings of Jesus (the word). Creation is groaning looking for solutions to climate change, terrorism, economic crisis and suchlike, but my understanding here is that let us look for the owner of this planet and petition Him of the problems we have at hand, and I believe He will be the best person to fix it. This is wisdom.

If you are lost and do not know what to do in this life, just touch the hem of His garment (the word of God).

If there are problems, burdens beyond your control, do not hesitate to touch the hem of His garment.

Jesus created everything; He has the power to fix everything. That is why He said in Matthew 11:28 "come to Me, all you who labour and are heavy laden, and I will give you rest."

He is waiting for you so come!

CHAPTER 8

THE REALITY OF GOD'S GRACE

Beloved God is so beautiful to the extent that His inconceivable and incomprehensible love towards man is beyond description. Once Dr. Creflo Dollar said, "The gospel of grace is too good news to be truly good news." And that is the manifold wisdom of God towards man. The grace of God towards man means God does not want any soul under this sun to perish and therefore, has made every provision for man to be saved, protected and prosper.

God's Grace

The word 'grace' in Hebrew is "Chen," which has two pictographic Hebrew letters.. ..The first is "Chet," which means "fence" as a fence is erected to protect a property. The second pictographic letter is "nun," which means "fish." This letter is commonly associated with life since fish lay hundreds of eggs from which springs forth much life. Thus, combining the two pictographic letters gives us a word that conveys the thought of PROTECTING LIVES. So, the word grace in the Old Testament means God's protection upon His people. The Hebrew word "Chen" is also closely related to the word "chanah" which is most often is translated tent or encampment, and we know that the purpose of a tent is to protect the lives of the people in the tent.

Beloved let us look at the first place the word "Chen" in the Bible.

"So the Lord said," I will destroy man whom I have created from the face of the earth, both man and beast, creeping thing and birds of the air, for I am sorry that I have made them, But Noah found grace in the eyes of the Lord."

— Genesis 6:7-8

God was going to destroy mankind except Noah and his family because Noah found grace (Chen) in the eyes of the Lord and therefore, God was going to protect his life.

"Then Lot said to them, please, no, my Lords! Indeed now, your servant has favour (grace, Chen) in your sight, and you have increased your mercy which you shown me by saving my life; but I cannot escape to the mountains, lest some evil overtake me and I die."

— Genesis 19:18-19.

Lot was having difficulty figuring out what to do as he saw hell breaking loose, so God protected him and his family by picking them up and placing them outside the city. The favour (grace, Chen) protected Lot and his family's life.

"For the Lord God is a sun and shield. The Lord will give grace and glory; No good thing will He withhold from those who walk uprightly."

— Psalm 84:11.

God is our strength and shield; He will give (grace, Chen) and glory to those who walk in His righteousness.

We see from the above scriptures that (grace, chen) is to protect life, and that God is the protector of the believer. But grace has another aspect that is closely related, and that is the thought of being favoured. When Jacob was returning to the land of Canaan and met his brother Esau on the way, he separated his children by their mothers, but kept Rachel his favourite wife at the back. He protected her most. We are the same way. We love our children, and when we see them going the wrong way or getting ready to make a bad decision we want to step in and protect them, because we do not want them to get hurt. Our children get this protection because they are our children, but we do not often extend the same concern to our Neighbour's children. God favours those He loves, those who please Him, and those who join in covenant with Him. He often does this simply by building a hedge, a wall of protection around them just as He did to Job.

Grace In The New Testament

The Greek word for grace is "charis" which means:

Unmerited favour of God.

Undeserved favour of God.

Unearned favour of God.

Once upon a time in the garden of Eden, the scripture says man committed a very high treason against his creator and deserved nothing but death, but God who is rich in mercy, with His inconceivable love decided to forgive man. The scripture says even when we were enemies and sinners, He still loves us and brought us to Himself through Jesus Christ, something that even the angels cannot fathom. The book of Psalm chapter 8:4 says, "what is man that you are mindful of him, And the son of man that You visit him?" The scripture again says the wages of sin is death, but the gift of God is eternal life in Christ Jesus our Lord. God could have whipped mankind from the surface of the earth for disobeying Him, but He decided to save and protect man hence His grace (Chen), and not only did God spare man's life but also to share with Christ's glory. That is to say, we do not receive what we deserve (mercy), and we receive what we do not deserve (grace).

At this point, let me use scripture to explain vividly the grace mentioned in the New Testament, and you will know and understand that God is really beautiful.

The Prodigal Son

"And the son said to him, Father, I have sinned against heaven and in your sight, and am no longer worthy to be called your son. But the father said to his servants, "Bring out the best robe and put it on him, and put a ring on his hand and sandals on his feet. And bring the fatted calf here and kill it, and let us eat and be merry."

— Luke 15:21-23

This prodigal son admitted that he had sinned against the father and the word of God, so he pleaded for forgiveness and that the father should not consider him as a son but one of his father's servants. Amazingly the father did not only accept him as a son but shared with this prodigal son the family's wealth. The father could have rejected and thrown him out of the house but chose to accept him and even shared the family's glory with him which even irritated the senior brother. Due to the love that the father had for the son, mercy accepted this prodigal son, and grace gave him what he did not even expect, and that is how our Heavenly Father's mercy and grace works towards us. Long ago even before the foundation of the world, God chose us to be His very own through what Christ would do for us, and God decided to make us holy in His eyes, without a single fault and we stand before Him covered with His love, all because of His mercy, grace, and love towards man.

The Woman Caught In Adultery

"When Jesus had raised Himself up and saw no one but the woman, He said to her "woman, where are the accusers of yours? Has no one condemned you? She said, No one Lord." And Jesus said to her, neither do I condemn you, go and sin no more."

— John 8:10-11.

According to Deuteronomy 22:22, this woman who had committed adultery was supposed to die, and knowing what was going to follow next ran to Jesus with her accusers holding stones ready to stone her to death. These accusers were ready to apply the law accordingly without mercy as this woman laid prostrate at the feet of Jesus. It was, therefore, a horrific scene, it was a life and death situation, and her last refuge and hope was Jesus. Immediately God's love showed up, and within the love was mercy and grace to save and protect this poor woman's life. God is beautiful indeed!

Jesus, Bishop Of Souls

"And when His disciples James and John saw this, they said Lord, do You want us to command fire to come down from heaven and consume them, just as Elijah did? But He turned and rebuked them, and said" You do not know what manner of spirit you are of. For the Son of man did not come to destroy men's lives but to save them. "And they went to another village."

— Luke 9:54-56.

Jesus one day sent messengers to one of the villages in Samaria to reserve rooms for them, but the scripture says the villagers refused to have anything to do with them, meaning they rejected and prevented Jesus from entering their village. It was then that James and John suggested to Jesus to allow them to command fire from heaven to consume the people, but Jesus rebuked them expressing His sharp disapproval to the suggestion. "You do not know what manner of spirit you are of. For the Son of man did not come to destroy men's lives but to save them." Jesus was trying to explain to them that the Spirit at work at this dispensation is called "The Spirit of grace," and His work is to save and protect lives and not to destroy them, and therefore any person who has not got a message that saves and protect lives better keep quiet. The message of the Spirit of grace ought to be nothing but Edification, Exhortation, and Comfort, as stated in 1 Corinthians 14:3.

Kinds Of Grace

In 1 Peter chapter 4:10, the scripture says God's grace is of manifold, such as:

The Saving grace.

The grace to teach and to preach.

The grace to conquer and to overcome.

The grace to be rich.

The grace to be strong.

With these manifold grace deposited in man, there is no way a believer should fail in this life. Let me confidently say that it is inappropriate, spiritually illegal, and against divine order for a believer to fail. Let me explain this.

"And lest I should be exalted above measure by the abundance of the revelations, a torn in the flesh was given to me, a messenger of Satan to buffet me, lest I be exalted above measure. Concerning this thing, I pleaded with the Lord three times that it might depart from me. And He said to me," My grace is sufficient for you, for My strength is made perfect in weaknesses." Therefore, most gladly I will rather boast in my infirmities, that the power of Christ may rest upon me. Therefore, I take pleasure in infirmities, in reproaches, in needs, in persecutions, in distresses for Christ's sake. For when I am weak, then I am strong." 2 Corinthians 12:7-10.

The great Apostle Paul who laboured more than all the apostles had a thorn in the flesh, so he pleaded with the Lord to remove it, but the Lord declined. God had a reason for that; and the reason was that the Lord did not want Paul to be exalted above measure. The Apostle was made known to many revelations, visions and mysteries, and the Lord did not want pride to take the better part of Paul, like Lucifer who went wayward after God Almighty has decorated him and placed him above all the angels. God in His own wisdom, allowed the messenger of Satan to operate so that Paul could depend on His sufficient grace, which has been made available for him. Some of us were so stubborn to the calling that God has to allow calamity to hit us to get our attention. When Paul understood God, he rejoiced in the sufficient grace which God has provided for him. The apostle understood that with the sufficient grace made available, persecutions, distresses, infirmities, and such-like against him will amount to nothing, and with that understanding, the apostle would not move an inch without the grace. He understood that without the grace, it was impossible to make a headway in life. He, therefore, made a profound statement in verse 10 of 2Cor.12 "For when I am weak, then I am strong." Meaning that though I am weak and vulnerable (a mortal man as I am) but because of the grace at my disposal, I am strong, and nothing could stop me from doing what I want to do to the glory of God.

Beloved the sufficient grace that God is talking about here is His power and might that He makes them available to save and protect His people. The same Spirit who raised Jesus from the dead is the same Spirit of grace whom God had made available for us. He is the Highest Ruler with authority over every other power. "How can this be?" Mary asked the angel, and the angel answered,"... the power of the Highest will overshadow you..." The power of the Highest is right there inside you, and therefore, impossibilities must not be entertained in any way.

Changing The Cable

With this grace available, there is no way for failure except by policies of consensus and compromise.

"For indeed the gospel was preached to us as well as to them; but the word which they heard did not profit them, not being mixed with faith in those who heard it."

— Hebrews 4:2.

When the children of Israel were told to go and possess the land flowing with milk and honey, the scripture says most of them could not make it to the land due to disobedience and unbelief.

"...But with most of them, God was not well pleased, for their bodies were scattered in the wilderness. Now, these things became our examples, to the intent that we should not lust over evil things as they also lusted. And do not become idolaters as were some of them. As it is written, The people sat down to eat and drink, and rose up to play. Nor let us commit sexual immorality, as some of them did, and in one day twenty-three thousand fell, nor let us tempt Christ, as some of them tempted, and were destroyed by the serpent, nor complain, as some of them also complained, and were destroyed by the destroyer. Now all these happened to them as examples, and they were written for our admonition, upon whom the end of the ages have come. Therefore let him who thinks he stands take heed lest he fall." 1 Co.10:1-12.

Upon all the miracles that God performed in Egypt and in the wilderness, the parting of the Red Sea, the miraculous water from the rock, and the manna from heaven did not change the children of Israel a bit. They still doubted the capabilities of God so the scripture says most of them could not make it to the promised land. God told them His readiness to protect their lives and also fight for them in all their battles, again God assured them of His blessing, yet the Israelites rejected their God who brought them out of Egypt, and they paid dearly for it. The scripture in Hebrews 4:2 says they heard the good news, but because they did not embrace it with faith (they compromised), the good news did not profit them.

Beloved the good news is that once upon a time, you were a sinner and an enemy to God Almighty, but now you are righteous because of what Christ

Jesus has done for you on the cross of Calvary-2 Cor.5:21, Romans 5:18-19. The good news is that once upon a time, you were rejected, thrown out of place, but now you have been reconciled back to God, and He is not imputing your trespasses to you because of what Christ has done. You have been made a king or queen, royal priesthood, a holy nation, and a unique person - 1 Peter 2:9. The good news is that you are blessed with every spiritual blessing - Eph.1:3, and have the mind of Christ - 1 Cor.2:16. Not only that, you are spiritually alive - Eph.2:5-6 and powerful to do all things -Philippians 4:13. You have been born again - John 3:3, a new creation - 2Cor.5:17 and sealed with the Holy Spirit of promise - Eph.1:13 and getting ready to be glorified - Romans 8:11. One needs to embrace all these with faith; else he will not benefit from any of them.

Renewed Mind

One, therefore, needs a renewed mind to receive and enjoy all that the good news presents, and the reason is, an old corroded cable cannot transmit power from a brand new Generator to the bulb to produce light. The spirit man (inner man) is born again, brand new creation without any blemish, the inner man is spiritually alive and strong, what is needed to manifest what is inside is to renew the mind.

> *"Beloved, I pray that you may prosper in all things and be in health just as your soul prosper."*
>
> **— 3 John 2.**

In November 2017, a pastor friend invited me to speak at their annual Conference on the topic, "The Lord will settle you." I told the congregation that the day they got born again was the day the Lord settled them, and I supported my statement with the above scripture. Beloved the truth of the matter is that the day you got born again, you became spiritually alive, God that day restored to you all the power and the blessing you lost to the devil in the garden of Eden. The inner man is settled, prospering and enjoying in his new status, but to manifest what is inside, we need to renew our minds and connect it to our born-again spirit. Your born again spirit could be likened to a brand new Generator with no-fault, while your body is likened to a living light bulb which is ready to produce light. Now, if the bulb (body) cannot produce the light then automatically, the fault comes from the cable (the mind). The logic here is that, as a corroded cable cannot transmit power from a generator to a bulb to produce light, so also a doubtful mind (an old mind) cannot transfer things from the spirit.

Unbelief and doubt are such dangerous spirits, I personally consider them as the most dangerous of all. These spirits are saying God cannot do what He has promised. When a squatter promise you five thousand dollars and you know he is a squatter, you will not believe because you will doubt his financial prowess and because you doubt, you will not believe all that he told you. In a nut-shell, he is a liar that is why you doubted him. When we doubt all that God has told us, we are literally saying He is a liar, and if He is a liar, then He is not God, but we have only one liar and the father of lies who is Satan. Beloved renew your mind (believing all that God had said concerning your life) after that, connect your renewed mind to the spirit, and you will be glad you did.

CHAPTER 9

LOCATING YOURSELF IN PROPHECY

"Before I formed you in the womb I knew you; Before you were born I sanctified you: I ordained you a prophet to the nations."

— Jeremiah 1:5.

The scripture records that there was a prophetic word on Jeremiah's life even before he was born as a prophet to the nations. If Jeremiah had decided to become anything other than what he supposes to become, he would have failed dismally. He would have moved away from the prophecy and the purpose for which he was created. Whenever we try to change God's plans for our lives, we work against ourselves; the reason is that God has our best interest in mind. "For I know the thought that I think towards you, says the Lord, thoughts of peace and not of evil, to give you a future and a hope."- Jeremiah 29:11.

When we fail to locate ourselves in prophecy we are bound to suffer; we become candidates of suffering. When you were in your mother's womb what was the prophetic word concerning your life? What does God want you to do and where does He want you to be?

"Your parcel is waiting for you at where God wants you to be." Let us make a mental illustration to help understand the scenario better. God created Smith to be a teacher and positioned him in Ghana, and before God created him, He had already made provision for him over there. Smith parcel had already been packaged and placed in Ghana as a teacher because that is what and where God wants him to be and accomplish his divine purpose. Due to pride, selfish desire or self ambition, if Smith finds himself in another country, Smith would be carrying out a failing experiment of his life. The reason is that he has moved away from God's purpose and the prophecy on his life. Frustration will definitely dominate his life because he has failed to identify his place and purpose on earth, and any time a person fails to locate himself in prophecy, he misses his parcel too. Many are in this situation and have attributed their frustration and failure in life to their parents, family members and friends. Some have even called their family members witches and wizards and belief that they are the direct cause for their set back in life.

How To Locate Yourself In Prophecy

What do you want to do to help your family and society which you have not done, and it saddens your heart all the time to the extent that you get angry for not being able to accomplish that task.

> *"Now it came to pass in those days, when Moses was grown, that he went to his brethren and looked at their burdens. And he saw an Egyptian beating a Hebrew, one of his brethren. So he looked this way and that way, and when he saw no one, he killed the Egyptian and hid him in the sand."*
>
> — Exodus 2:11-12.

What Makes You Angry

Moses, a Hebrew but raised in the palace by Pharaoh, one day went to visit his brethren in the field and saw a Hebrew been beaten, this made him angry, so he killed the Egyptian to save his brethren. Moses after that escaped to Midian because Pharaoh heard what he had done and wanted him to be killed. Forty years later, God called Moses and assigned him to go back to Egypt and deliver his brethren from slavery. This was something that he already wanted to do but he could not because he was operating ahead of prophecy at that time. Anger brings ideas, changes and innovative strategies. It simply increases our passion and until you get angry and hate that situation, you cannot bring about the needed change. Anger can also bring about destruction, and that is the negative side of it, which Satan uses to destroy that which God has done or want to do.

What Makes You Sad

"......I took the wine and gave it to the king. Now I had never been sad in his presence before. Therefore, the king said to me why is your face sad since you are not sick? This is nothing but sorrow of heart. So I became dreadfully afraid and said to the king, may the king live forever! Why should my face not be sad, when the city, the place of my father's tombs, lies waste, and its gates are burned with fire?"

— Nehemiah 2:1-3.

Nehemiah became sad when he heard that his brethren back home were in distress and the wall of Jerusalem was broken down with its gates burned with fire. King Artaxerxes then asked Nehemiah the cause of his sad demeanour, and after he had told the king everything, his request was granted. Opportunity was given to him to go back to Jerusalem and embark on his wish, fulfilling the prophecy in the book of Jeremiah 29:10. Most often, it is the love, mercy, and compassion the person has towards the situation that brings about the sadness, and this sadness, which is deep in the person's heart, causes him to change a bad situation. When one considers the shortest quotation in the bible, "Jesus wept" John 11:35, one will realise that the love and the compassion that Jesus had for the Lazarus family caused Him to be sad and wept. The scripture says after that Jesus went to the tomb and changed a bad situation there. That sadness when it hit your heart 'pump' will cause you to fulfil prophecy. The love and the compassion that Jesus has for man saddened His heart, which caused Him to come and save man down here on earth. Do you feel sad in your spirit because some people are not saved? Rise up and fulfil prophecy.

Your Desire

Whatever you desire to do, whatever you always wanted to do, you were born to do that thing. Check the things you love doing best and you do them with joy. As a student, check the subject that you perform well at school, and most often, they are the subjects your interest lies. Do not forget that your desire should always bring glory to God. A person's desire should also bring inner peace and comfort to him or her, for if fear, anxiety, and tension reign in your heart concerning that desire, then one needs to pray for clear cut direction from God. Such a situation two things may come to mind, either the devil is playing tricks with your mind, or that desire is not of God for your life. Let me clarify with the scriptures.

In the book of Judges 14:1-6, the scripture says Samson had the desire of getting a wife from a town called Timnah, in the land of the Philistines. Though it was of God, the enemy in a form of a lion came from nowhere to put fear and panic into him, just for Samson to abort his heart desire, but the Spirit of the Lord came to his rescue. Every God's dream, vision, purpose or assignment will always attract the devil; that is why it is necessary to depend on God and be in tune with His Spirit against any deception.

On the other hand, it was good for king David to build a temple for God, but God prevented him and said his son Solomon should do it. Though the desire was a perfect one, God did not approve it. In all these, we should allow the word of God and the Holy Spirit to guide us, locate ourselves in prophecy. Let me suggest the following to you:

1. Study the word of God with regard to your situation.
2. Pray over it using the scriptures.
3. Meditate on the word of God you used to pray and the Holy Spirit will bring a clear-cut direction to you after this spiritual exercise, but if still you do not get it, then you may seek counselling from brethren. You can also contact me.

Grace, Protection, Favour, And Victory

Success is the accomplishment of a divine purpose. Any person who locates himself or herself in prophecy is guaranteed of a divine grace, protection, favour and total victory.

Grace

The scripture says king Saul sinned against God and therefore was dethroned as king of Israel. I have a question here, did David sin when he was on the throne? And one day David broke about five of the Ten Commandments, but God referred to David as a man after His heart.

Referring to Genesis chapter 49:10, "The scepter shall not depart from Judah nor a lawgiver from his feet until Shiloh comes. And to Him shall be the obedience of the people."

There was a prophetic declaration upon Judah by Jacob, and that only the tribe of Judah was mandated to produce kings in Israel. Now Saul was a Benjamite and therefore, he was not aligned with the prophecy because of that God's grace was not upon him. God chose David as a king of Israel from the tribe of Judah fulfilling prophecy in Genesis 49:10, because of that the favour of God was upon David. When a person locates himself in prophecy, that person enjoys God's grace, and that grace covers him even when he slips. Have you been chosen by God? John 15:16, and are you fulfilling prophecy? Then you have that same grace upon your life. Hallelujah!

Divine Protection

John Wesley said, "I am immortal until my work is done." When a person locates himself in prophecy that person becomes immortal, that person enjoys God's protection day and night. Did you know that Moses' first attempt to deliver the Israelites failed? Moses has to run to Midian because his life was in danger for killing an Egyptian. Moses was moving ahead of prophecy that said the Hebrews would be in slavery for four hundred years, then God will deliver them. Moses' second attempt was successful because he was then operating in prophecy, and was getting all the backing from God. The scripture says Moses took ashes and blew them into the air which resulted in a plague in Egypt in the very presence of Pharaoh but the king could not raise a finger against Moses. The reason was that Moses was operating in prophecy getting all the divine protection from God.

Once a woman came to narrate a dream she had about me and that one of these domestic birds (cock) wanted to harm me with the beak, but suddenly, a tall man from nowhere came and put his arm around my shoulder and we vanished. She was overwhelmed when she was narrating the dream, but I told her to hold her peace. " Because the Lord is with me as a mighty terrible warrior. Therefore, my persecutors will stumble and will not prevail. They will be greatly ashamed, for they will not prosper. Their everlasting confusion shall never be forgotten." Jeremiah 20:11.

An Uncommon Favour

There is an uncommon favour that God carries out on anyone who locates himself in prophecy.

"And a letter to Asaph the keeper of the king's forest, that he must give me timber to make beams for the gates of the citadel which pertain to the temple, for the city wall, and for the house that I will occupy. And the king granted them to me according to the good hand of God upon me. Then I went to the governors in the region beyond the river, and gave them the kings letter. Now the king had sent captains of the army and horsemen with me."

— Nehemiah 2:8-9.

Israel has been in exile for seventy years, according to the prophecy in the book of Jeremiah 29:10. Now after the seventy years, God set them to return to their homeland, and Nehemiah, who was the king's cupbearer, was the leader of the second batch of people who returned from exile (Persia).

The first batch to come was led by Ezra, who rebuilt the temple, and the third batch was led by Mordecai. Nehemiah who had the compassion and the passion for going back to Jerusalem and rebuild the broken wall, requested from the king building materials. The scripture says because God's hand was upon him, all the requested materials were given including horsemen who guarded Nehemiah's journey back home. Nehemiah went to Persia as a slave but left Persia as a king, all because he was on God's assignment. As you purpose in your heart to be part of the kingdom builders, may God supply you with the necessary materials you need. May God grant you an uncommon favour, may He bring you into the company of people you need to know and into the knowledge of things that you need to know that are critical to your success, destiny, and purpose in life. May you begin to live as a king and queen all because you have located yourself in prophecy and fulfilling it.

Victory

"Then Joshua said, open the mouth of the cave, and bring out those five kings to me from the cave. And they did so, and brought out those five kings to him from the cave: the king of Jerusalem, the king of Hebron, the king of Jarmuth, the king of Lachish, and the king of Eglon."

— Joshua 10:22-23.

The tenth and eleventh chapters of the book of Joshua record a total victory for Joshua. Five kings joined their forces together against Joshua in battle, but they could not prevail. Beloved the truth of the matter was that Joshua located himself in prophecy; he was on God's assignment. All the kings in the world could have put their strength together against Joshua, and that would not have worked either because it was time for the children of Israel to enter into the promised land, and nothing could stop them and God's purpose.

"For the Lord of Hosts has purposed and who will annul it? His hand is stretched out, And who will turn it back?"

— Isaiah 14:27.

Tasting God's Power

Let us draw an example from the book of Esther. Esther was a slave girl in a foreign land, Persia, so how did she become a queen? God had prophesied, and who could have disapproved of God's plan? It seems difficult and impossible with man, for a slave girl like Esther becoming a queen in a foreign land but with God, it is possible. God behind the scene orchestrated everything making sure that He uses queen Esther to fulfil His purpose. Haman who was manipulated by Satan thought he was fighting against man, little did he know that he was fighting a losing battle with God, in the sense that Esther and Mordecai were just vessels that God was using to fulfil what He had declared. The seventy years in exile which the prophet Jeremiah declared in Jeremiah 29:10, needed to be fulfilled, and when a person is fulfilling prophecy, no one or power can stand against it. Do not be afraid, walk in faith and in victory, and never think that you walk alone. Let the devil and his demons know that they cannot touch you because you have located yourself in prophecy and fulfilling divine agenda.

My Conversion

"Many are the plans in a man's heart but it is God's purpose that will prevail."

— Proverbs 19:21

This means that God's purpose is powerful than man's plans.

God's purpose is important than man's plans.

God's purpose first before man's plans.

After my tertiary education, I did one year National Service. My plan afterwards was to travel to the United States or Europe to make ends meet, so I gathered all the necessary documents needed to acquire a visa from the embassy, but unfortunately, I was denied a visa. Some months later, I went to the Netherlands embassy, and there too, I was refused the visa, although I spent a lot of money, but it yielded no results. I became frustrated and did not know what to do next. I then decided to earn quick money, so I entered into gold business, but because I had no knowledge in that, I failed dismally. I tried other businesses, but they yielded nothing positive. Anything good I touched turned bad, and life became a living hell.

One morning my mother who knew my predicament, suggested that I enrol in a bible college. As a matter of fact I did not like the idea. I did not understand why I should become a pastor and live on people's offerings. I thought that the pastoral work was reserved for the frustrated people in life. I considered pastors to be the disappointed in society, but little did I know that it was my calling. God's purpose for my life was to preach His word to the broken hearted, but there I was making choices that were worsening my already bad situation. Many are the plans in a man's heart, but it is God's purpose that will prevail.

On September, 1990, my sister went to be with the Lord and at that moment of mourning, God woke me up from my sleep around 2am and said, "son listen attentively, give your life to me and I will give you rest else you will die miserably." Fear gripped me and I did not know what to do. As early as 5am, I was behind one pastor's door knocking, and he led me to Christ. From there, I went to stay with a cousin for almost a year and prepared myself for the bible College just as my mother suggested to me earlier. I was awarded a 1st Degree in Theology and was ordained as a minister of the gospel on March 14, 1993. I was posted to pastor a church, and I serve the Lord with all my heart. In 1994, I organised an international crusade with the main speaker from the United States in the person of Dr. Roger McPhail. The purpose of God was fulfilled because His power was manifested in various ways.

An Invitation To Switzerland

I had an invitation to minister in Switzerland, so I gathered a few documents, including my passport, and went to the Embassy for a visa. I reached there late, but I was able to hand over my documents to the consular officer, "Reverend, please bring your two passport pictures and your air ticket for your visa." I could not believe that it was going to be that quick. Some years back, I had spent so much money on a visa but could not get it. God's purpose is always important and powerful than our plans indeed. My experience before I got converted could be equated to Jonah in the Bible. Maybe you feel you are sinking in distress but know that with Jesus in the vessel, you will soon smile at the storm. All you need is to repent and run to Jesus the Saviour of the world. He says, "come to Me, all you who labour and are heavy laden, and I will give you rest." Matt.11:28. Pastor John L. Mason said, "you can never see the sunrise by looking to the west."

Purpose Orientated Dream

By purpose orientated dream, I am referring to those who have located themselves in prophecy and are fulfilling them. Those who are on God's assignment. These people have dangerous dreams, visions, and assignments, also they are the most powerful and dangerous people on earth, in the sense that they are too tough to be handled. Bullets fired at them are like straws and lay a hand against them, and you will remember the battle again no more. You cannot tame or stop such people. Remember that these people are those who have located themselves in prophecy and are fulfilling them. Such people have the full support of heaven. Let me prove my point by scripture.

> *"So the Lord said to Moses: see, I have made you as God to Pharaoh, and Aaron your brother shall be your prophet."*
>
> — Exodus.7:1

Catch a revelation here and put it within your heart for there is going to be a lifting up of your head, and all the doubting 'Thomases' will see it and marvel. I would like to remind you that as you locate yourself in prophecy and begin to fulfil that divine prophecy, you have been made as God to your enemies.

Those who want to keep you in slavery will be greatly ashamed, they will stumble and fall, they will not prosper, and they will not prevail, their everlasting confusion shall never be forgotten. God told Moses I have made you as God unto Pharaoh, whatever you say to him, he has to obey. In Exodus 12:30-36, the scripture says the Israelites were favoured by the Egyptians, and they plundered them before living Egypt. After Israel had left Egypt, Pharaoh and his horsemen chased them, but eventually, they perished in the Red Sea because the power that Pharaoh and the Egyptians were dealing with was too powerful and dangerous for them to handle.

Beloved, the same Moses who became boss over Pharaoh had earlier escaped from him to Midian because Moses murdered an Egyptian and hid him in the sand when he tried to save the life of a Hebrew in the field, and this brought problems to him and has to run away for his dear life. The question here is who assigned Moses to go and deliver his brethren at that time? Or was it his own curiosity that brought problems to him? At that time, God had no business with him and had not been chosen for any assignment of that sort, for the four hundred years bondage in Egypt was not over yet. Mathematically the prophecy at that time was three hundred and sixty years old. It was after forty years in Midian before God called him in the desert to assign him.

You have been chosen to execute a specific assignment for God, and therefore you are God's ambassador, representative, an envoy of Heaven on earth. The name of your ministry is called "The Ministry of Reconciliation," and you are the minister in charge. You are so special to God at this moment that any spirit, power, or person who touches you unlawfully will regret, and as God was with Moses, He is also with you. As Pharaoh and his horsemen perished in the Red Sea, even so, shall Satan and his demons perish. Greater is He who is inside you than he that is in the world. "Indeed, they shall assemble, but not because of Me. Whoever assembles against you shall fall for your sake." Isaiah 54:15.

This reminds me of the day Saul who became Apostle Paul, went blind for three days when Jesus arrested him on the road of Damascus for persecuting the church. "Saul, Saul, why are you persecuting Me?" Anyone who jokes with you or the church is treading on dangerous grounds because the church is Christ, and Christ is the church. Just be part of the church, be on the campaign trail and execute your assignment accordingly and the enemy has no business with you.

Joshua Account

"Then Joshua spoke to the Lord in the day when the Lord delivered up the Amorites before the children of Israel, and he said in the sight of Israel: Sun, stand still over Gibeon; And moon, in the valley of Avalon. So the sun stood still. And the moon stopped, Till the people had revenge upon their enemies. Is this not written in the book of Jasher? So the sun stood still in the midst of heaven, and did not hasten to go down for about a whole day. And there has been no day like that, before it and after it, that the Lord heeded the voice of a man, for the Lord fought for Israel. "

— **Joshua 10:12-14.**

Joshua was the first leader to enter into the promised land with the people, but then he has to fight these nine feet Anakims, the Canaanites, Amorites, Jebusites, Perizzites, and all the 'ites' who were occupying the land. At one point, Joshua told God to let the sun stand still till he has finished destroying the enemies, and God hearkened to a mortal man like Joshua, and the reason was that he was on God's assignment.

"When your plans fit into God's purpose, victory is inevitable."

When a person identifies his or her purpose on earth and begins to fulfil it, the person becomes like God Himself, because the person is in a sensitive mission which is divine. The person becomes God walking among men on earth, and that is God in operation using human flesh. In Joshua chapter 11:4-8, the scripture says the enemies that came against Joshua were like multitudes, as many as sand at the seashore, but what happened to these enemies? God dealt with them decisively.

Jehu

One of the remarkable miracles the Bible recorded was that of Elijah at Mount Carmel. Elijah, after that great event, went to hidings because Jezebel threatened to kill him for slaying the prophets of Baal. God, therefore, anointed Jehu and assigned him to go and kill the woman in Jezreel, and it was so simple that when he entered Jezreel, he went straight to the palace and ordered the eunuchs around her to throw her down from the upstairs through the window. No war songs, no gunshot, neither was there a resistance from the queen, this was because the power of God that was in Jehu paralysed the woman to the extent that she could not pose a resistance.

Mordecai

"That night the king could not sleep. So one was commanded to bring the book of the records of the chronicles; and they were read before the king."

— Esther 6:1

Mordecai was a Jew and a security officer at the gate of the king's palace in Persia who refused to salute Haman, the Prime Minister, and because of that, Haman decided to kill him and the Jews. He then sought permission from the king which was granted, so a date was set to annihilate all the Jews who were in the king's provinces. The night before the destruction, Haman, his wife, and friends planned how Mordecai ought to be killed. The scripture says, that same night whilst they were planning Mordecai's death, the king was also contemplating how Mordecai has to be rewarded. Early in the morning, Haman was to pick Mordecai from the palace gate for execution but first wanted to greet the king, and as he entered, the unexpected happened to him. The king asked Haman, "What shall be done for the man whom the king delight to honour?" Now Haman thought in his heart, "Whom would the king delight to honour more than me?" Haman then answered and said, "Your majesty, let a royal robe be brought which the king has worn, and a horse on which the king has ridden, which has a royal crest placed on its head. Then let this robe and horse be delivered to the hand of one of the king's most noble princes, that he may array the man whom the king delights to honour. Then parade him on horseback through the city square, and proclaim before him: Thus shall it be done to the man whom the king delights to honour!" "Go and do exactly as you have said to Mordecai," the king commanded Haman.

There was a swift turn of event, and how did it happen? The answer is simple. Mordecai was fulfilling a prophecy that went forth in Jeremiah 29:10, and that the Jews will be in exile for seventy years and after the seventy years are completed God will cause them to return to their homeland, but Haman at the other end was challenging God's word, and decided to annihilate Mordecai and all the Jews, and this was ridiculous!

"When Haman told his wife Zeresh and all his friends everything that had happened to him, his wise men and his wife Zeresh said to him, If Mordecai, before whom you have began to fall, is of Jewish descent, you will not prevail against him but will surely, fall before him."

— **Esther 6:13.**

It was Haman, Mrs. Haman, and the wise men (their friends) who planned how Mordecai was going to die, but surprisingly Zeresh, Haman's wife and the friends now turned around to advise Haman he cannot prevail against Mordecai because he is a Jew. When one follows the story carefully to Esther 7:10, he will find out that the gallows that Haman and his people prepared for Mordecai were the same gallows he was hanged in. All those who fight against God's word and His purpose are fighting a losing battle, and it is very dangerous to touch a man who is fulfilling prophecy.

Have you located yourself in prophecy, and are you fulfilling it? If the answer is yes, then you are the most dangerous person on earth. On the other hand, if you have not, then try and identify it, because when you were in your mother's womb, there was a prophetic word concerning your life. Identify that divine purpose and locate yourself in it, and success will never elude you. It's a principle of God.

CHAPTER 10

GIFT

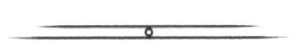

A brother one day asked me if the continent of Africa is cursed, but I told him no. God loves Africa the same way He loves the rest of the world.

A Christian woman also once narrated to me her desire to offer unto God good tithe and offering and also help the needy, but she is financially handicapped and therefore cannot do what she intended to do. She then asked me to help her in prayers." What do you do for a living," I asked her? "housewife," she replied. I asked her again if she is paid for being a housewife and the answer was no. This woman's gift has not been identified, nurtured, and polished, therefore she cannot be a blessing to society as she had wished. I told her I was going to pray with her and surely, God was going to speak and direct her to find her purpose in life. To God be the glory, this woman is making it big in business.

One day I asked a brother why many people, especially Africans usually buy second-hand goods, and the answer was that they are cheap. Why do they buy cheap, used goods? Because they do not have money and cannot afford the brand new. Why are they financially handicapped? Because they are doing menial jobs, and why menial jobs? It was a very interesting, sensitive and thought-provoking discussion, and we learnt a lot after the discussion. We found out that many Africans have not identified their divine purpose in life (the reason why God created them); others have found them but are not polished enough (not well developed) to benefit the society. God did not create Africans empty, and no one came to the world empty-handed, we need to identify our gifts and develop them, and it is a principle of God.

Africa leads the rest of the continents in terms of Christian population, yet poverty is so high. As Christians, we suppose to command wealth because we have the mind of Christ, which presupposes that as Christians, we have the knowledge and the wisdom of God. All other things being equal, the world should have depended on the church for direction, wisdom, and wealth because the church has the mind of Christ, we are also blessed with every spiritual blessing, but we rather see the opposite. Africa is supposed to be one of the richest continents because of its Christian population. In 2 Corinthians 8:9, we can see that Jesus Christ though He was rich, became poor so that we Christians might become rich. Again in 3 John 2, we Christians have been made rich and prosperous in all things. Christianity means going back to the original. Original of what? Original of how God from the beginning created man in Genesis 1:26-28. When one gets born again, the person regains the power and the blessing that were lost in the garden of Eden. We are therefore blessed and have the power back to multiply and lead.

However, all these blessings and prosperity are packaged in our gifts. That is why Proverbs 18:16 says, " A man's gift makes room for him, And brings him before great men." In this generation, one can see young men and women who are millionaires through their gifts, especially these sports personalities. I sometimes hear some Christians praying for money, fine, nothing is wrong about that, but I would have loved if they could channel their prayers very well, that the Holy Spirit should help them identify their gifts, what they are made of, so that they can nurture and polish them to create wealth. The truth of the matter is, there are a lot of these millionaires who are non-Christians and therefore do not pray or embark on fasting and yet are rich. The principle here is, the gift of a man and that man the Bible is talking about could be a Christian or non-Christian. Brethren, we can fast for forty days or go beyond that but if we do not exercise our gifts we should forget it. Even if a gift is not exercised on a $50 million, it will amount to nothing. That is why Africans keep soliciting grants and financial gifts from donor countries to balance their Yearly National Budgets yet getting nowhere. A principle cannot be violated and go scot-free, and the principle is your gift (talent) will make you great.

In Matthew 25:14, talents (gifts) were given to three gentlemen, five, two and one. Two of these men worked with their talents, but the third one refused to have anything to do with his; eventually the one who did not bother to work with his talent was deprived of the one he had as it was collected and given to the more industrious one. In 2 Corinthians 9:10, the scripture says it is God who gives seed (not forest) to the sower, and in every seed is a forest. If that seed could be nursed and nurtured, it becomes a forest. If that gift (talent) that God gives to each and everyone, before he or she was born is nursed, nurtured and polished it becomes attractive and beneficial to the person and society. It is a principle laid down by God (The Creator of the universe), and Africans cannot run away from it. God in His own wisdom has blessed Africa with much gifts, seeds (human and natural resources) but we are sitting on these resources without polishing (developing) them, and because nothing is seriously being done about it, the continent has automatically become borrowers, beggars, and parasites (a dumping place for the advanced countries). I believe in prayer and fasting, but every door has its key. The key to financial buoyancy is through the gift that God has given to man.

Do you believe that God created some to be great and others to be poor to the extent that daily bread is a problem? Do you believe God created some continent to be special and others inferior? What brings about poverty, dependency, borrowing, low self-esteem and such-like?

I believe that all men were born in the image and likeness of God and therefore, all men were born special and great. All men were born with a gift, and this gift is given to man like a small tiny, fragile and unattractive seed. Satan knowing this most often attacks these gifts at its youth state, and that is when the youth engage themselves in all kinds of social vices, and at this stage, the young do not sometimes know what he or she is going to become in the future.

God also gives gifts such as natural resources to nations and it is the duty of the nationals to identify, develop and protect these resources, but failure to do so will send the entire nation into slavery, becoming slaves in their own land. In a situation like this, the nation becomes a parasite, beggar and liability to the society.

The Reality Of A Gift

1. When a gift is not identified, nursed, and polished, the person becomes a dependent, a liability to society, a parasite and a beggar at the same time. That person loses his or her dignity, honour and respect.

2. Once the gift is destroyed, the person becomes a walking 'confusionist' on earth.

3. The gift of a person defines his or her real meaning in life, just as God used Esther's beauty which is also a gift to save a whole nation. Esther became a queen in a foreign land though she was a slave, but her beauty pushed her there. God working behind the scene used Esther's position as a queen to accomplish His purpose. Beauty is a gift, our women should use it judiciously to the Glory of God.

4. A destroyed gift cannot be used for God's purposes. If Esther had been sleeping around, her beauty would have deteriorated, and God could not have used her for His purpose.

5. God's given gifts are always small (like the mustard seed), fragile and unattractive from the beginning but when it is nursed, nurtured, and polished (developed), it becomes attractive to benefit society.

6. Every gift from God is precious, unique and dynamic. The gift of a medical practitioner or a legal practitioner is equally good as a farmer or a barber, the only question here is about the polishing. If the farmer or the barber can polish his or her gift, the person could make financial gain out of it.

7. Society will continue to despise you including your wife, until your gift is identified and polished.

8. Until a gift is nursed, nurtured and polished one cannot benefit from it because it does not help society in any way.

9. A gift when polished attracts multitudes; it opens doors, and it brings the person before great men.

10. Nothing can liberate a person or a nation from financial turmoil until that person or nation has brought the developed gift to bare. No amount of donations from the IMF or donor countries can solve the economic problems of a nation or individual. It has been years since Africa started receiving donations, grants and financial support from the advanced countries, yet poverty reigns supreme in Africa. Until we get fed up with poverty, rise up and develop our God-given gifts, we should forget it entirely. This is a hidden truth.

What Do You Have

"So Elisha said to her, what should I do for you? Tell me, what do you have in the house? And she said, Your maidservant has nothing in the house but a jar of oil."

— 2 Kings 4:2.

No one was born empty, for there is something precious inside you that God is going to use to perform a miracle out of it for His glory.

A widow in a serious financial crisis who did not know what to do. The husband had died leaving a debt behind, and all indications point to the fact that the family did not have enough to live on, and as she ponders over all these things, her creditor comes for his money and failure to settle the debt would send her two sons into slavery. A situation that sometimes one finds himself in, which most often needs God's intervention, so the scripture says this woman ran to the man of God for a solution. The prophet asked her a question, "what do you have in the house?" This widow first answered "Your maidservant has nothing in the house," The widow was indirectly telling the prophet, that jar of oil in the house cannot solve the problem at hand, she despised the little oil in the house. Precious one, with humility, I can boldly say that every tiny seed from God potentially is a forest. Jesus Christ told Jairus do not be afraid, only believe, and she will be made well. There was going to be a miracle of abundance for this widow, but then God needed something little He could use from her. Do not despise that little gift but trust in God, nurture and polish it, and sooner you will be with great men.

From Prison To Prime Minister

"Then Pharaoh said to Joseph, Inasmuch as God has shown you all this, there is no one discerning and wise as you. You shall be over my house, and all my people shall be ruled accordingly to your word; only in regard to the throne will I be greater than you. And Pharaoh said to Joseph, see I have set you over all the land of Egypt. Then Pharaoh took his signet ring off his hand and put it on Joseph's hand; and he clothed him in garments of fine linen and put a gold chain around his neck. And he had him ride in the second chariot which he had; and they cried out before him, Bow the knee! So he set him over all the land of Egypt."

— Genesis 41:39-44.

I believe that you know the circumstances that led Joseph to prison. Now after all the challenges, the disgrace and the humiliation that the young man (slave boy) went through, he eventually became the prime minister of Egypt. Who did it? God! By what means? Through the gift of the young man, and what was the gift? Dream interpretation.

God caused Joseph to occupy that high position, but He used a gift to do that. The scripture says not even Pharaoh's wise men or the magicians could figure out Pharaoh's dreams, and therefore had to bring Joseph from prison. At that moment, everything came to a standstill with the spotlight on a Hebrew young man's gift, which God gave to him when he was in the mother's womb. The gift of a man the scripture says will open doors for him and bring him before great men. Beloved, no one can perpetually make you free except your God-given gift, and it is a principle that every Christian and Africans should be mindful of. I know certain communities in Africa who work on lands which legally are not theirs, they have sold the lands to expatriates, and the sad news is that they could not utilised the proceeds well. Why? Their gifts were not acted on it.

The Sling Of David

"So Saul clothed David with his armour, and put a bronze helmet on his head; he also clothed him with a coat of mail. David fastened his sword to his armour and tried to walk, for he had not tested them. And David said to Saul, I cannot walk with these, for I have not tested them. So David took them off. Then he took his staff in his hand; and he chose for himself five smooth stones from the brook, and put them in a shepherd's bag, in a pouch which he had, and his sling was in his hand. And he drew near to the Philistine."

— 1 Samuel 17:38-40.

God needed a sling and a smooth stone to accomplish another miracle to save the children of Israel from the hands of the Philistines in the battle. God did not need a helmet of brass or coat of mail, neither did He need a sword.

Though David was a brave warrior, he had not proved himself with those weapons, and if God had wanted to use the armour, He would have used king Saul to accomplish His purpose, but since Saul had been rejected, he has to use David and what he is made of. Now, if God wanted to use David, then it should be a sling and a stone because inside David was a sling and a stone and not Saul's kind of weapons. You better put it down if it is not meant for you, but sometimes due to pride, greed, and vainglory, we choose things that are not meant for us and experiment with our lives on them. God will always use what He has given to you. The way Goliath was dressed who thought a sling and a stone could kill him? Be content with the gift that God had given to you and thank Him and never despise a gift for every gift is unique and dynamic. I have seen high profile businessmen such as gold dealers who lost their lives because they ran into serious debts all because it was not their field of operation. There is this woman who operates in a restaurant somewhere close to the city and as early as 7am customers begin to queue up for food, and the interesting thing is that some of these customers come from a great distance. This woman is successful in the business, and the secret is that she is operating in her gift. All God's gifts are perfect, dynamic and unique, so do not discriminate any. Identify yours and develop it (polish it). God is not dead, He is not far away from you, and He is not partial but loves you the way He loves everyone, except that His principle says your financial buoyancy is in your gift.

Shalom, God's peace be with you.
Daniel Asihene.

www.ingramcontent.com/pod-product-compliance
Lightning Source LLC
Chambersburg PA
CBHW030258010526
44107CB00053B/1752